STILL HERE

AND STILL

STRUGGLING

TO SERVE

GENA B. McCOWN

End Game Press books may be purchased in bulk at special discounts for sales promotion, corporate gifts, ministry, fund-raising, or educational purposes. Special editions can also be created to specifications. For details, contact Special Sales Dept., End Game Press, P.O. Box 206, Nesbit, MS 38651 or info@endgamepress.com.

Visit our website at www.endgamepress.com

Hardback ISBN: 978-1-63797-062-1
Paperback ISBN: 978-1-63797-069-0
eBook ISBN: 978-1-63797-063-8
LOC: 2022939873

Published in association with Michelle Lazurek of the Word Wise Media Services.

Cover Design by e210 Design
Interior Design by e210 Design

Printed in India
TPL
10 9 8 7 6 5 4 3 2 1

With my deepest love and appreciation to my husband and children for making the space, so that I could be exactly who God created me to be.

CONTENTS

ACKNOWLEDGMENTS 3

FOREWORD *by Holly Cyr Cain* 5

INTRODUCTION. 9

CHAPTER ONE *Over 50 Years of Struggle* 23

CHAPTER TWO *40 Years Later* 33

CHAPTER THREE *Struggling with History* 45

CHAPTER FOUR *Struggling with Feminism* 61

CHAPTER FIVE *Struggling Scripture* 75

CHAPTER SIX *Struggling with Semantics* 91

CHATPER SEVEN *Struggling for a Seat* 109

CHAPTER EIGHT *Struggling with Hope* 127

CHAPTER NINE *Don't Take My Word for It* 139

AFTERWORD 161

ACKNOWLEDGMENTS

To my best friend, Aimee Nelson.
The one who calls me brilliant when I feel less than,
and affirms me when the world tries to shut me down.

My gratitude to the women who have shared their
stories with me, trusted me with their pain, and imparted
their hopeful wisdom to this work. I write for us.

My deepest appreciation to the leaders who have invited
me into their spaces, made room at their table, and
blessed me more than I could ever bless them in return.

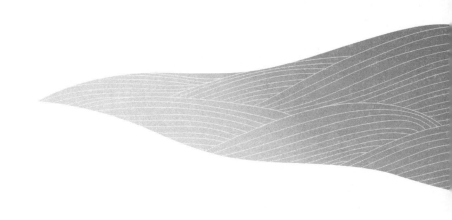

FOREWORD

I'm shocked at how many times the story of the woman who anoints Jesus with perfume has shown up for me recently. It started a couple of months ago and it has gotten more frequent since then. Since it didn't seem like it was going away, I decided to read the story in all four gospels.

Whether you believe this is one story written from different angles or four distinct events the basic storyline is the same: a woman breaks into a dinner party, cracks open a very expensive bottle of fragrance over Jesus' feet, and the men at the table cluck their tongues in disbelief at her audacity.

I imagine her finding out Jesus was in town, figuring out where he was, gathering her most expensive offering, and rushing to where he was. In my mind when the servant answers the door she doesn't even converse with him but pushes her way past to see Jesus. I bet she didn't even look around the room. I assume she found Christ's face in the crowd and bee-lined it to his side. My thought is that this happened so fast that some guests smelled the perfume before they even realized she was there or what was happening. I think she was probably a weeping mess, a broken but intent worshipper. I bet the only person she knew was in the room was Jesus. I'm sure she heard the scoffers but her attention never wavered.

I love this story. I love the woman's disregard for who might be in the room. I love the urgency you feel. I love her single-minded focus. I love her devotion.

Most of all, though, I love Jesus standing up for her. I love that he accepted her sacrifice and saw her for who she was. I love that he had to explain to the men in the room what she was doing because they didn't even get it. I love that she was part of the bigger narrative of salvation and that Jesus said she would be remembered throughout the world for what she had done.

This story hits home for me in so many ways because I sometimes feel like this woman: not invited to the party, no place at the table, not like anyone else who has "arrived", sneered at for misusing my gifts, and chided for not doing what is acceptable to the religious. I so resonate with her position.

But I also resonate with her desire too. All she cared about was her proximity to Christ, her ability to be completely spent for his service, she was blind to what others thought, and she had complete trust in Jesus to protect her.

This story exemplifies Our Struggle to Serve and Still Here to a T. All we want is the ability to serve our Savior with the very valuable gifts he has given us, to be broken and poured out at his feet, and to have a singular focus on his greater Kingdom purpose.

It boggles my mind that we are still in this battle, that we still need to remind people what we know and where we've been. I had this discussion with Gena over dinner not that long ago. I said, "I feel like when I walk into a church I need to bring my resume so that people know that I know what I am doing." It's not even from a place of "look at me" but rather "don't discount me". We lamented over educating ourselves, putting in the time, putting in the hours, and getting our hands dirty week in and week out and still not being seen for what we have and want to offer.

On the podcast I co-host, "The Christian Woman Leadership Podcast", we have been interviewing Christian women leading in ministry or business for over 3 years and it is interesting to me the amount of those women who have sought leadership outside the walls of the church because that is where they are valued for their contributions. They are more quickly paid, promoted, validated, and developed inside of boardrooms and cubicles than they are in pews. They are fulfilled and following their calling in places and spaces not generally occupied on Sunday morning.

In line with Gena's sentiments in the pages to follow, yes, this gets a rise out of me and makes me want to fight the patriarchy, but more than anything I am grieved for the Church. When more than 50% of its body is discounted or crippled how can we expect to be effective? When those long-time female attenders feel marginalized, what relief can they offer newcomers who are searching for hope? Where is the realization of the freedom offered through Christ when half of us are chained to "biblical womanhood"?

In this masterful work, Gena truthfully guides us through the realities faced by many women in the church today. She respectfully and objectively paints a picture that is hard to look at but is nonetheless what the body of Christ needs to face. Most of the tones of this reality can feel somewhat gray, but layered behind these bleak strokes are vibrant colors of women who serve through their gifts nonetheless. Women who despite the scoffs minister to the least of these. Women who in the face of criticism still show up even though their professional training tells them they could be leading things more effectively.

Gena is the bold yet wise truth-teller we need. She meets confusion and divisiveness with a plain and simple perspective that is hard-won. Every time I talk with Gena I walk away inspired by her love for the church, her ability to love without bitterness, and her genuine hope that we can push the needle forward in this lifetime. She is committed to developing women in leadership but mostly she is dedicated to Christ and his kingdom come. I'm in awe of her knowledge and perseverance for the women of Christ. I can't think of a better person to have written this book.

In the chapters to come, you will come face to face with the struggles and challenges we still wrestle with every Sunday.

If you are a man and you are reading this, I want to say thank you. I ask that you read with an open mind not discounting our stories as singular one-offs. I can tell you that for every story Gena conveys in each chapter there are 10,000 more that could be told and for every experience detailed at the end of this book there are 100,000 more that could be outlined if only there was no fear of repercussion or setback. This is happening in your church.

If you are a woman who has struggled to serve reading this, hear me when I say you are not alone, you are not crazy, and your leadership matters. I hope in these pages you find comradery and validation but most of all please hear the overarching theme that you were created to glorify God and he made and gifted you on purpose for a purpose.

The book you hold in your hands is pivotal for the church today. We need to grapple with its pages and chapters in a new and more courageous way. We need to see, really see, the treasure we have in front of us in the women sitting in our pews. We need to crack those most valuable treasures open and pour them at Jesus' feet. They need to be used to glorify God as a sweet aroma of his grace.

Holly Cain
Founder of Prosper Collective and co-host of The Christian Woman Leadership Podcast

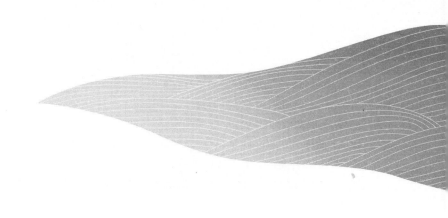

INTRODUCTION

About ten years ago, I attended a conference by The Gospel Coalition. Just a few days prior to the conference I received an invitation to a special event for women who were interested in seminary education. I had already received my Divinity degree, however I was considering exploring further education options; so I signed up to learn more about the schools and their programs.

The room was packed full of women, to the point that the tables and chairs had long been filled and women circled the room seated on the floor. Several women were standing in the doorway. At the front of the room stood a panel of representatives from several different seminaries. They decided the most effective way to address the questions of the crowd was to pass the microphone around the room. Each woman was instructed to ask her most pressing question related to seminary, and then pass the microphone along. The questions were categorized to allow the representatives to respond more efficiently during the second half of the meeting.

This was a very wise format, as I am certain they anticipated many of the women would have similar questions. It was evident that most women in the room were feeling called or nudged into further education. Yet, the stumbling block was universal: *Why should I invest my money and time in a seminary degree when there doesn't seem to be any place for me to use that degree vocationally?*

As the seminary representatives tried to answer this question with an impressive list of suggestions, there was an air in the room that I could only describe as disbelief. In retrospect, when I consider their suggestions, I still feel disenchanted. I personally know too many women, with seminary degrees, that have been unable to find employment in ministry. Without a doctorate, finding a teaching position in any higher learning environment is nearly impossible even with decades of ministry experience.

This was not the TGC Women's Conference, where the crowd is predominately women; but the TGC National Conference, where the attendance is almost exclusively men in Pastoral or staff roles within their local churches or ministries. I attended these conferences for the leadership investment, even though I wasn't nor ever felt a calling to be a pastor. The number of women in attendance was surprising to some of their presenters. I recall attending a workshop on Systematic Theology, and the session leader commented on his surprise and pleasure in seeing so many women signed for it.

Yet, here were all of these women eager to learn. Filling up the workshops on theology, doctrine, and interpretation. Taking fastidious notes on Bible study techniques and ministry acumen. The call was present, the desires of their hearts aligned, but a strong hesitance to sign on the dotted line of a seminary application. As I walked through the exhibition area, considering my own next steps in education, I made eye contact with a gentleman who was manning a seminary booth. I approached to inquire about more information and informed that this particular school didn't accept women as students. However, I was welcome to take one of the free pens.

Tides have been turning for quite some time. Women are interested in deeper understanding of the Word. There are more Marys delighted to sit at the feet of the Teacher than Marthas concerned with housekeeping and setting out a Pinterest-worthy meal. Theologically educated women are on the rise, yet the amount of vocational positions for these women has barely moved the needle.

Then it is no surprise that when presented with an opportunity to discuss seminary education, the women would question to what end? What would be the purpose? What is the return on that investment? When I told my own family that I was returning to school for a divinity degree, the recurring question was: *"what are you going to do with it?"*. And, discouraged, I would reply: *"I have no idea. But God is calling me here, paved the way, and I must be obedient."* Thanks to the internet, the opportunity to educate oneself is nearly limitless. However, obtaining the formal education with accompanying diploma feels restrictive due to the capping of opportunities once graduated.

With over two decades of ministry service, practically full time for most of that, under my belt and a degree, I still have been unable to attain full time employment in ministry. Within the last month, I reached out to a network of women who have at least two masters degrees or a doctorate about continuing my education. When asked if it was better to have a doctorate in the same vein as the first masters degree or to get a second masters degree in a different leg of ministry to broaden my qualifications, my motivation for continued education was questioned. I responded that I had hoped it would open the pathway for more employment options. To which every single woman told me to not bother, unless I was planning to become a college professor.

Not to bother.

A waste of time and money.

Audit classes instead.

Choose a cheaper certification.

Survey Says

I was disheartened by the response of my peers, but also spurred on to dig a bit deeper to understand the reasoning behind those answers. I sent out a survey to every single woman that I personally knew in ministry, as well as shared it on several public social media platforms. I wanted to know what mattered most in order for a woman to advance in her church in the area of leadership.

The options in the survey included:

- Having a personal relationship with the pastor (either directly, or indirectly through familial relationships).

- Establishing a long history of service/attendance in the church.

- Having a theological degree.

- Professional experience related to the particular area of leadership.

The results confirmed my peers' assertions regarding degrees. The value of a woman having any sort of theological degree or professional experience was negligible toward increasing service opportunities, leadership, or employment. In fact the overwhelming response was having a personal relationship with the pastor, with established history in the church a distant runner-up, was your best course of action to get anywhere.

Naturally, when one sees the results of a survey question, other questions begin to arise. I wanted to understand how trust was built in those relationships with the pastor, which would result in its taking precedence for advancement. My assumption was that discipleship must be involved. These pastors must be developing women as leaders via discipleship, so that they felt confident in their theological training sans degree. Additionally, this discipleship would also ensure that the women would have an understanding of the exact mission of the church, and the particulars of that church's culture.

I surveyed the same women about their experiences being discipled in the church. The options given in the survey included:

- The church automatically paired me with someone for discipleship/mentoring.

- I asked the church for discipleship/mentoring first, and it was provided.
- I asked the church for discipleship/mentoring, and was denied. I had to seek it on my own, outside the church.
- I have never considered or been offered discipleship/mentoring.

To my absolute dismay and utter disappointment, I was stunned that over 50% of the surveyed women said that they asked for, but were **denied**, discipleship/mentoring, instead having to seek it on their own. Can you imagine? Asking your pastor to disciple you, or connect you to someone else who could... and being told no.

Then is it any wonder women have begun turning outside the church to build up their leadership chops? Is it any wonder that women in the church are still struggling to serve, when no matter how hard they try to prove their qualifications, they are dismissed? Is it any wonder that churches may have a history of poor female leaders if the precedent for leadership is *friendship* over *qualification* via education or experience?

Not to mention, how can we call ourselves churches that follow The Great Commission, when we have people asking for discipleship and being denied. The very thing that The Great Commission calls us to do. Go forth. **Make disciples.** Baptize them. Teach them.

A Reflection on Struggling

I shouldn't have been surprised by any of the survey results. Their responses were my responses. I suppose what I desired from the surveys was affirmation that my story was unique, hoping that it was just circumstances holding me back, not my gender. I truly did not want to believe that we were still struggling to simply serve. The survey indicated that this was not generational, geographic, or even denominational, but a lingering shackle from which evangelical women have been unable to shake free.

Women are not just struggling to find jobs. They are struggling to lead, and even simply serve in their gifting as volunteers. Women still feel like they are overlooked and undervalued. Fear binds women into complacency because boldness comes at great expense.

Over my lifetime, due to moving, I have attended several churches. As I reflected on my own experiences, I began to notice consistent things that just simply didn't make sense. When my husband and I moved to a new city, we would visit a few churches, select one that fit our family best, take the new member class, and plug in—attending small groups, events, and our children attending Vacation Bible School and youth. In short order, I would start exploring areas to serve.

To date, there has never been a single pastor or church leader that met with us. No one has ever asked about our educational backgrounds, faith story, or even what our spiritual gifts might be. No questions were asked about our theological training. The closest might have been in filling out the membership form, if there was even a section to account for our personal testimonies. There are a lot of ways we could have served our churches over the years, but no one ever asked us... because they didn't know what we had to offer. Too often by the time we would become aware of an area that we could help or offer expertise, there was no interest or room for added voices.

I never thought that I should attach a copy of our professional resumes to our membership applications. It never occurred to me that I should drop an email to the pastor outlining our gifts and talents, and how they could help within the church. Nor, had I ever considered the need to provide our life's curriculum vitae of faith. We just waited for the pulpit announcement declaring help was needed in a particular area, made note of where the sign up sheet was, or whom to contact for more information.

It amazes me that in the process of onboarding new members; there is no process for getting to know who these people are, learning their education or professional background, assessing their spiritual gifts, and then connecting new members into areas to serve. As leaders, we wait for people to just randomly volunteer. The members, are waiting to be invited. It's a stalemate between two sides of the same game. And, women are still fighting to even play.

One particular day, my husband was on an extended medical leave. Our pastor, at the time, called to speak with my husband. We were in the midst of a huge renovation project at the church, and the pastor figured my husband had some time on his hands to help with some research. This happened to be an area that my husband had zero experience in. Calling me over, I overhead him say, "You might want to talk to Gena about that. She's practically an expert. I wouldn't even know where to begin."

My husband handed over the phone, the pastor brought me up to speed, and within seconds I rattled off a litany of questions for him. Things my husband would have never known to ask, and by his response I don't think the pastor had even considered. Within 48 hours of getting those answers, I had set up appointments for quotes, resourced information on some secondary options, and drawn up a floor plan that incorporated various options depending on the aesthetics they desired.

There have been so many occasions over the last several decades, where I felt as if I could have saved the church some time, money, and from serious headaches. Women can be visionaries as well. We can see the big picture. Our experiences help us to see down the road, around the corner, and up the next block. We do think differently, and that can be a blessing to have a different point of view. Women can also serve as administrators that help visionary leaders put their ideas in to action.

Just as much as we should be concerned that theologically trained women, or professional women, are overlooked in areas that are related to their expertise, we should be equally worried about the number of women that are assumed to be good at something just because of their gender. As a woman, I recollect all of the times I was allowed to lead in an area where no one bothered to vet my doctrinal beliefs being aligned with the church, my qualifications to lead in that area, or even my personal walk. There was a hole in the organization, I was a warm body, and I willingly raised my hand to assist.

When it comes to mothers' ministries, women's ministries, women's Bible studies where we are pressing start on the video and following the leaders guide... there is little oversight. Just because I am a woman doesn't mean that I am the right fit for the nursery or children's ministry. Nor does being a woman guarantee that I can whip up food for an event, or that I have the eye for decorating the narthex.

I recall being in church one afternoon when several staff members and their wives were having an informal lunch meeting. One of the wives chimed in, "*I think if parents are using the children's ministry, then they need to volunteer to serve a certain number of times per year in that area.*" I couldn't help but overhear, and speak up. I explained that if it came to that, I would have my children sit in church with us. Children's ministry just was not part of my gifting. The wife couldn't believe her ears! She quickly retorted: "*But you are a mom.*"

Yes. I am a woman. I am a mom. I love my children. I believe I have done a great job teaching and raising them. However, I am not gifted as a teacher to other children. I have never felt the call to children's ministry. Although, I will happily fill in for a nursery worker who calls in sick at the last minute. Not every woman is naturally gifted to work with children. The same can be said of hospitality or other domestic duties. For some women it is as natural as breathing, for others it is a real struggle.

As church leaders, we need to be building up relationships with our members. Learning of their gifts and talents, professional experiences, and then translating that information to determine where they best fit in the service of the church. In smaller churches with limited staff members, this might be too much to take on due to already overwhelming responsibilities. Just as much, it might be too big of a job for the megachurch pastor with tens of thousands of members. However, if we put the right systems into place... and expand our leadership teams, even as volunteers... we can lift that load of the pastor's shoulders.

The sobering truth is that I am a woman who struggles to serve. Even now. Getting the degree, didn't make a difference. Traditionally publishing a book, didn't make a difference. Establishing a history of regular attendance, commitment, and dedication to my church... also didn't make a difference. No one had bothered to really get to know me or the breadth of what I could offer.

So, I tried to adapt. I said yes more, without questioning or challenging. I supported the vision of the church entirely. I rallied the troops when changes were coming to embrace these new adventures versus fear them. I was the biggest cheerleader. I changed how I dress to fit the look of the church. I showed up early. Did the work. Stayed late. Proving my worth. Establishing myself as a team player. I was 100% on board with the plan.

I buried my head when I was disrespected. I didn't point out the times where my suggestions would have helped the situation, but were ignored. I didn't defer to my expertise, but yielded to the male leader with less experience out of respect for his authority. I was not going to fight for a seat at the table but instead keep showing up and perhaps one day I would be invited. I essentially embraced an attitude of taking what I was given. Like a dog, grateful for the scraps that fell from the dinner table.

He watched as I restrained myself and held back. My husband has held the tear stained face of his bride. Once full of life and vigor, now a shell of her self afraid to rock the boat, even when she could see the waves coming. He would champion me to push harder, as I pushed back suggesting we just needed to be more patient. My children watched my struggle, and as women they saw the underlying message.

It didn't matter.

There was no place for women here.

Our gifts and talents were dispensable.

It is incredibly conflicting to be called a high capacity leader, who is quick to adapt, and performs above and beyond expectation... and yet, from the same leadership to be dismissed, disrespected, and even forgotten.

It brings me no joy to say these things. Writing this book is painful, as I relive some of the most heartbreaking moments of my ministry service. But, I would be remiss to leave this world without being part of the needed change. Perhaps undoing some of the damage that my daughters have witnessed.

As a woman of resolve, I couldn't bring myself to just exist in this world and contribute nothing back for the Kingdom. So, like many female leaders before me, I took my gifts into the world. I began developing, mentoring, equipping, and supporting women in ministry leadership. My utmost desire was to do this under the authority of my church, but at that point I couldn't even get my pastor to meet with me. I would be for the next generation of women the very thing I longed for. I would provide opportunities for their leadership skills to be honed and exercised.

Over these last ten years, I have struggled to see any improvement for women in leadership. In fact, quite the opposite. I began to notice a decline. The women I connected with were growing more frustrated. While some denominations, or independent churches, had begun to open doors for women beyond nursery care and hospitality... others were closing doors. I have witnessed the slow death of Women's Ministries; the already small pool of areas women could serve, without any controversy or debate are diminishing.

The Search for Hope

I needed to find hope. Hope that there were opportunities out there. Hope that things were improving, even when it didn't feel that way.

Seeking some sort of reassurance that there were places where women could serve, in the fullness of gifts and calling. The research began. I felt as if we must be missing something, a key to unlocking the shackles, releasing that anchor dragging behind us.

Books were ordered. Articles downloaded and printed out. Highlighters, pens, and notebooks strewn across the desk. Podcasts were subscribed to. As I consumed all of these resources, it was apparent that many seemed to be supportive of women in expanded leadership roles, even if Pastor was still off the table. Yet, reality didn't seem to match. It was altruistic.

Within my surveys, many woman lamented that the written policies of their churches, regarding women, didn't seem to match up with their actions. Due to an unwillingness to put their money where their mouth was, women who found themselves in 100% agreement on paper were considering leaving their churches due to inaction. The proof was in the proverbial pudding.

With women comprising 30 - 40% of seminary students, it is evident that the same percentage of ministry jobs are not being filled by women. In my own quest to find full time employment in ministry, the options are so limited that almost all would require uprooting my family. I often do not learn of job openings in my church, or local community, until it has already been filled. Or, I since I was automatically disqualified as a woman there was no reason to inform me that the position existed. After getting my Divinity degree, I logged on to some employment board sites for churches in order to see what was out there. My church had three active job postings. I didn't even know we were hiring.

Jobs that are available for women are often at a lower pay rate, which makes relocation incredibly difficult (particularly when she has a well-employed spouse). The chances of equally or out earning a spouse, at this point, is so slim that relocating has become a non-starter. When such a job does appear, where relocating is a possibility due to the compensation package, the number of women vying for the position is a deluge. I have received emails from churches thanking me for submitting my resume, but due to the "overwhelming number of inquiries they are no longer accepting applications".

I continued searching for the silver lining. When, to my husband, I proposed an opportunity that was local enough, but would require my entering into essentially a two year preparatory school (similar to seminary), including an internship, and employment was not a guarantee... he laughed at the notion. He asked, *"What more do you have to do, to prove that you are qualified?"*

As I kept searching for that glimmer of hope, I came across the book, *Our Struggle to Serve: The Stories of 15 Evangelical Women"* by Virginia Hearn. It was published in 1979. The stories predated the publication, as early as the 1920's. If anything could show me where the needle had moved, it would be this book.

There was a need for something concrete to grasp, to encourage the endurance to keep running the race. As I passed through the pages, my heart grew dim. I recognized my own struggles in these stories. Women were pouring out their pains and I grieved along side them.

Yet, despite the struggle, they had the very thing that I was searching for. Hope. They witnessed that there was an air of change. The tides were shifting. Opportunities were becoming available. These women were the trailblazers, and they knew it.

"You and I will never experience the fruits of this movement; we are only emerging "persons". It will be better for our granddaughters, when it is accomplished, but now it's only a start.

Such responses reveal how much progress still is needed before Christian women can recover the sense of self-worth inherent in being made "in God's image". Is progress possible for the women in today's evangelical milieu? My own life – and the lives of the courageous women who tell their stores in this book – show that it is." *(Our Struggle To Serve, Virginia Hearn, 1979)*

In doing the math, I realized I am the granddaughter she spoke of. I found myself crying out to grandmother Virginia in lament. I needed her wisdom. Tell me how to fix this. I'm weary, and still struggling to serve. *We* are still struggling, as women, to serve.

CHAPTER ONE:
FIFTY YEARS OF STRUGGLE

When Virginia Hearn set out the parameters of her project, it wasn't easy. In the decision to tackle this project, she understood that including the accounts of other women would be pivotal. Reaching out to her contemporaries, she looked beyond a single denomination or cultural background, balancing the progression of the book between seasoned women and those who were emerging leaders the 1970s.

Twenty five letters were drafted to her peers and contemporaries. Outside of Virginia's own account, only fourteen others were willing to contribute to the work. This was one of the first areas that I felt a kindredness with Virginia. When I reached out to women in my surveys, the majority of them were happy to participate in helping me collect data. However, they did not want to be interviewed or provide anything that could be a quote attributed directly to them; hesitation lay in providing too much information. The reasons I was given were not far from those Virginia received.

Women were afraid to speak up about their struggle to serve in the evangelical church. It was impossible to contribute to the project, while skirting certain facts that would easily identify those involved. Details, memories, and stories were so specific they feared an inability to even contribute anonymously. Women feared back-lash from the public, their churches, and even within their own families. Participating could result in doors of opportunity being shut in their faces, and impeding the ability to make a real differ-ence. Fear of having their personal lives put under the microscope for public scrutiny weighed upon their decision making. Would failures or trials in their lives be trumped up to acting outside of the will of God because of their position?

Women didn't want to share their stores out of fear it would depress the readers, or out of a desire to not relive the pain they had experienced. Women feared that their words would be lost in the battle ground of feminism that was rising in the 1970s, or twisted and used against their advancement. Virginia writes, *"When I asked each of them to contribute her own story as a chapter, I encountered an incredible amount of fear, uncertainty about personal identity, and inability to get something down in black and white." (Our Struggle to Serve, Hearn, 1979)*

Turning page to page, reading through their accounts, you could simply replace a few dated words and equally believe that these stories were not from history but present day. The very ar-eas in which they struggled to serve or in regard to leadership, and their fears of challenging these norms, are not far removed from our own. Their fears remain ours. In my own attempt to solicit con-tributors to this work, I faced even more hesitation than Virginia. The struggle remains and the stakes are high.

The Role of Women

It was in the 1970s that the rising feminist movement pressed against the post world war conventions about a woman's place being in the home. While the men were off at war, women kept the country moving, taking on jobs that would normally be reserved for men. Once the men returned home, the expectation was to resume their jobs and the women retire back into their domestic duties.

Women found that they enjoyed employment and found fulfillment in serving a purpose outside the home. Having balanced home and work during the war, they didn't see any need to give up their employment. Women began to reconsider college education and vocational training. Those in unhealthy marriages found that employment provided the financial assistance they needed to strike out independently. Some women staved off the expectations of marriage and children to pursue a career. These women were already challenging the established norms.

By the rise of the feminist movement of the 1970's, women were pushing those ideas further. Fighting for equal rights, greater opportunities, and personal freedoms. This was significant change, and change threatens what society has grown comfortable with. While there were some men who supported expanding women's rights and fought for equality, others bucked against feminism to protect their status quo. This was exemplified in both society and within the church.

The women in *"Our Struggle to Serve"*, mostly lived not just in the thresholds of the 1970's women's liberation movement but in the decades prior. Their stories expressed similar themes. Women feeling as if they were second-class citizens in comparison to men. Less freedom. Less opportunity. For the vast majority of the women, society established that marriage and children as the highest priority in the life of a woman. The church made it her highest Biblical calling. The future of the Kingdom was dependent on her ability to bear children that would be raised in the church and carry the Gospel message to the future generations.

The accounts of the women hailed from the United States, Caribbean Islands, United Kingdom, and beyond. The expectations on women were seemingly universal; she would marry young, start a family. She may be permitted to continue her education, but it was expected that she would find her husband while in school. His education would supersede hers. If one had to quit school, it would be the wife. If they didn't marry while in school, it was expected to follow shortly after graduation. She may be permitted to work initially, but under no circumstances should she continue education or working once children entered the equation.

These were the expectations of society at large, and within the church; women were to be homemakers. Of the contributors who shared accounts of employment, it was universally indicated that there were few career paths open to women. Her options were secretary, cashier, waitress, teacher, or nurse. With the unwritten rule, that upon her pregnancy, she would quietly retreat into her new role of mother and homemaker.

The end of the war invigorated women's desire to pursue education and find a career. However, opportunities were limited and women were still overlooked or completely excluded from certain fields. They pressed forward, the numbers of women joining their ranks grew. Women's liberation was in full force. Society was shifting with it. According to the accounts in the original text, society may have been advancing, but the church was anchoring deeper in the mud and unwilling to be moved.

Opportunities for women in the workplace began to open up, they were feeling more welcomed as fellow students in academia, and the societal pressures to marry and have children were being lifted, or at least allowed to be delayed for a period of time. There was more autonomy in their lives, and the women felt alive. Yet, in their churches the environment was entirely different.

Many women felt as if they were living a duality between their daily life and their church life. Freedom to grow, learn, and lead in the workplace. Women were leading teams, making decisions, and walking more confidently in their skill sets. Equally feeling constrained in their churches by domesticity. Sitting quietly. Not asking too many questions. Definitely not challenging anyone in authority. Growing theologically at home, and playing the simple housewife at church.

Most of the stories, in *Our Struggle to Serve,* recounted being taught from a young age by their church leaders that their greatest calling was to marry and raise children. Implicating that The Great Commission didn't apply to women on a global scale, but fell within the teaching and raising of their children. Unless the women became missionaries, for which there seemed to be an unwritten exemption to the rule (so long as the women were not in their home country).

As a response to feminism bringing about change, change that threatened the norm, the church leaders of the time began using terms like "biblical manhood" and "biblical womanhood" to try and define roles to specific genders. Scripture was used to support those arguments, and women found themselves hard-pressed to challenge it. They were to accept their highest calling of marriage and motherhood, and that was simply that.

The older generations within in their families supported this ideal, it was this culture that they were raised in. Women and men felt the pressure from their parents and older relatives to fall in tow. Even the most progressive men, out of respect or reverence, didn't want to challenge their elders beliefs. Younger generations didn't have enough theological stamina to quite challenge it, and those who took the time to study were grounded in fear of consequences.

There was a battle brewing between three opposing forces. There were those who believed women could be more, those who wanted to hold to tradition, and those who were intentionally holding women back. Were the sexes totally equal in all things? Or, were they equal in many ways but also different? Did those differences disqualify women from certain roles? These were the questions of the time, and the same questions are still seemingly unresolved today.

Egalitarianism vs Complementarianism

It is almost impossible to believe that the words Egalitarian and Complementarian are still young words in the vernacular. Egalitarian (french for equality) didn't become associated with Christianity until 1984. Complementarian didn't enter the conversation until 1988, beginning as a term that was used as a brief descriptor of The Danvers Statement, which formally established in 1987 to set guidelines of the roles of men and women. It's from this ideology the book *Recovering Biblical Manhood and Womanhood* would be birthed. Still today, we find that in the boxing ring of women's leadership, it is Egalitarians in one corner and Complementarians in the opposing.

In the simplest of definitions, Egalitarianism implies that men and women are equal. There are no gender specific roles, the gifts and the callings of the Lord fall upon women and men alike. Essentially women can lead anywhere, including the church. There are independent, non-denominational, churches that have embraced this belief from their onset. Some denominations or conventions have embraced this view over time, making changes in small increments.

On the opposite end of the spectrum, Complementarianism implies that there are very specific roles for men and women. It takes an equal, but different approach. Suggesting that while we are alike in our Imago Dei (image of God) and equally valued by God, we have very distinct roles based on our genders to play out in the Kingdom story. This system puts limitations on which areas of ministry leadership are open to women, as well as limits men to adhere to certain gender stereotypes. Within the breadth of Complementarianism, there are some churches that have more restrictions than others. The topic of most debate is the office of Pastor, to which Complementarians believe is off limits for women.

Just as today, you can find people battling it out on social media and conference panels of the rightness of either camp, so could you equally find these arguments when Hearn wrote *Our Struggle to Serve*. At the time of publication, there were no fancy, multi-syllabic titles associated to the beliefs yet; nonetheless, they were views that were expressed, believed, and debated. A battle over *"what does the Bible really say"* about women in leadership has been waging for an incredibly long time.

By 1979, women were finally beginning to speak up against the accepted norms. Women were attending college, getting seminary educations (or equivalent of), and had a willingness to ask the questions and challenge interpretation. *Was the highest calling of a woman to be married and have children? Or, is there something more?*

A Limited World View

The crux of the issue, I believe, is that the arguments behind Egalitarianism and Complementarianism exist from a limited world view. Both are influenced just as much by opinion, interpretation, and society. The stories provided by these courageous women seem to share that view point. It's us versus them, and in the entirety of Scripture I can't find a support for that perspective.

Scripture reveals both women who were domestic and industrious. Women who were encouraged to be students, and those acknowledged as teachers. Women who were decisive, loyal, and strong. Equally women who were servant minded, comforting, and compassionate. My grandmother would tell me that there were always two sides to every story, and the truth usually fell somewhere in the middle. Scripture narrative reveals the many women who fell in that middle.

As I continued reading through the memories of these women, I was struck by their absolute dedication to the Word. Did all of the women agree to what degree women could serve? No. Yet, there was a consensus among them that there should be more opportunities than those to which they currently had access to.

Their stories were interwoven with the Scriptures they had tested popular belief systems against. A contentment would have been found in obedience to the Holy Spirit had their research revealed that it was merely the desire of their flesh to blame. This was genuine, deep, desire to not just get the answers they were personally seeking, but to be at one with the God of creation.

If there was work to be done, these women wanted to answer the call of "*who will go?*" If they were shirking their Great Commissioning, they wanted to rectify it by setting their hands and minds to the task. For the fifteen women who contributed to *Our Struggle,* this was their moment to blaze the trail for those coming behind them. They were fit for the task. Even if afraid. Even when they knew the cost was high.

From their perspective, they were just ascending the mountain. Knowing, all the while, that this journey wasn't just about their own future... but the future of the generations to come. These were our matriarchs, opening the pages of the Lord's Word and scouring it for His truths over man's opinion. This was no light task, but a burden for The Gospel. A reverence to rightly handle the Word of God.

We are not witnessing women who were fighting for the pulpit, but rather women who were clinging to the charge that the Lord commissioned to all of us. We are the hands and feet. We each have a part in this body, that helps it to function. Unique gifts given to us to do the good works we have been called to. There is a purpose for us in the advancement of the Kingdom. No one gets a pass. No one gets to sit out from participating.

Which makes it all the more difficult to compare their stories spanning forty to nearly one hundred years ago, to the struggle of women today. Bound by the same limitations. Taught the same highest calling. In my conversations with modern-day leaders, the same highest calling is being taught to women around the world. Taught not just by their churches, but their families as well.

It's central to the role of women in the quiver-full movement, to be a quietly submissive homemaker that bears many children. It's a common thread among many of the ultra conservative Christian homeschooling circles. A few years ago, one woman proposed to me that every family should have at least three children. Her reasoning was that the first two children would replace the parents in God's Army, and then the third and subsequent children added to the ranks. As if God's victory was dependent on us. Last time I checked, the victory was His at Calvary. Jesus alone is the one that overcomes.

In a conversation with my own children, I said something along the lines of *"if you decide to marry, and if you decided to have children..."*. My eldest stopped me before I could continue asking, *"Are you saying I don't have to get married or have kids, if I don't want to?"*. I had never taught my children that marriage was a requirement or expectation. Yet, somehow, whether it was the observing the world or some lesson in Sunday School, they were indoctrinated into believing this was their prescribed destiny.

The surveys I have conducted in preparation for this book indicate that even among the women successfully serving in ministry, that these struggles are still an issue for women today. Some improvements have occurred but more work must be done to open the doors for women. Women are still cautious and even fearful of speaking up or challenging the status quo lest they risk their jobs, their influence, and find themselves labeled troublemakers. Today's female leaders do not dare to speak out, because they know the cost is still high.

My email inbox filled with messages from the women who appreciated the work I was about to enter into with this book, but many apologized that they could only help so far. Spend any amount of time on social media platforms, following those who speak out for or against women in leadership, and you will be appalled by some of the behaviors.

We have witnessed it in how the evangelical world treated Beth Moore's open letter to the influential evangelical men who treated her poorly, her speaking up against injustice, and ultimately her exit from the Southern Baptist Convention. We bore witness to the reprehensible way that Aimee Byrd has been treated by the men and leaders in the Orthodox Presbyterian Church before and after her recent decision to lead the OPC. These women are not the first to stand up, but I believe it's fair to say that they can afford a boldness that the current emerging leaders, or the woman sitting next to you every Sunday simply can not. Don't let that imply they didn't bear an emotional and spiritual cost.

The women of Hearn's day were struggling to serve in the evangelical church.

Today, we are *still* struggling.

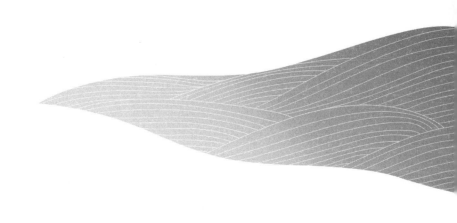

CHAPTER TWO:
FORTY YEARS LATER

As an adult, I entered into a professional workforce that was predominantly male. I was a young female with a vision of a future within the company; I had been warned that the pace for women's advancement in the marketplace can be slow and arduous. I was quite surprised to find that wasn't the case for myself. In fact, at the time of my last promotion, there were three openings which all were secured by women. By the time I left the company, I worked in a location where the entire management staff was entirely comprised of women.

Within just a few years, I had been promoted seven times. Just prior to my exit from the company, I was part of a team that trained all future managers within the company. I was overseeing a staff of nearly two hundred employees, as well as tens of thousands of dollars in sales per day at our location alone. I was very thankful that within this company, and those whom mentored me, that my gender did not disqualify me or hold back advancement. I returned to college, full time, to complete my degree in order to secure more options for my future.

It was during this time, that I became more invested in my service of the church. I had more time on my hands, and realized that much of the training and development I had received in the secular marketplace could be beneficial to my church. I was great at writing policy and procedural manuals, with an ability to see the project's vision into future. Meaning that from an administrative position, I could take the vision of the church or ministry, and follow it down the pathway it was heading. This would result in better preparation, anticipation of needs, and stability of the ministry model long term. When we can foresee the problems, we can get ahead of them before it becomes a real issue (responding versus reacting).

I met with one of the pastors to offer my services, and I began overseeing one of the subministries while faithfully serving for several years. In this time, I was able to create a procedural manual for the administrative functioning of the ministry. My goal in this position, as it was in my secular career, was to create a system that I could easily be replaced. Should I move on to a new ministry, whomever was to follow should be able to pick up the baton and run with it.

This was an amazing experience that set the tone for my expectations of my ministry future. My family relocated, and I was eager to find a church in which I could plug in and serve. Within about six months, I found the church where we would spend the next ten years. In that time, as a leader, I found myself extremely limited. There was only so much I could do, and my gifts of administration and leadership were mostly unnoticed. When job opportunities presented themselves, I was never even considered. Even with the leadership role I held, I realized quickly that I didn't have any real authority. As the leader of an entire ministry, I was never invited to attend a staff meeting nor involved in discussions of vision casting. I was really just an executor of their plan, my input didn't matter.

In the beginning, because of my history, I figured this was because the leadership didn't know me well. I hadn't been a member long enough to prove my worth or value. As time passed, I began contemplating that it was because I was lacking in something. While attending a conference, I made the decision that I should invest in a theological degree of some sort. Perhaps this was the missing link, the thing that would show the church leaders that I didn't just have administrative acumen but also theological knowledge. Yet, that didn't seem to matter. Degree in hand made little difference in how I was viewed.

The more I tried to prove and assert myself as a worthy leader, the more I was pushed away. Ultimately, as the result of a series of events, we made the painful the decision to leave that church. It was in that moment, that I thought that perhaps the issue with leading in the church had nothing to do with me. It was just that particular church. In the years, since, I realized I was partly correct.

In the book *Church Refugees,* researchers Packard & Hope recognized that the majority of the "Dones" or "dechurched" are people who were do-ers in the church. These were long term, invested members, who are known for getting things done. Ultimately, they have faced so much difficulty in serving within the church in the areas of their passions (or grown weary over church politics) that they have been driven from their churches in order to heed obediently to their calling. *"In short, the dechurched are people who do things, and without them, the church comes perilously close to losing relevance for people who want an active and engaged faith." (Church Refugees, pg 26)*

Not everyone wants to just sit among the pews, collecting dust, as they sit through another Sunday sermon and then quickly usher out the doors. Women, like me, are seeking to be active and involved participants in the church mission. Not consumers. Not witnesses. Not audience members. A person can only face rejection so many times before they will gather up their gifts and talents and leave. Leaving ultimately provides the freedom to be obedient in their calling, but leaving also comes with great pain, and even guilt. *"There is pain in the leaving. There's loss. But there's hope, too. We're able to do things now." (pg 26)*

It became abundantly clear, over time and observation, that it wasn't me. As in specifically me. The issue was that I was part of a church denomination that only made room for women to a certain level. Anything beyond that was out of touch, out of reach. So it was not me, it was my gender. At this point, I want to be clear that I am not addressing the Pastorate. I have never felt called into the Pastorate, but definitely felt called to use my administrative gifting as a leader within the walls of the church. Statistically there are more women leading (or attempting to) in other areas of ministry than Pastoral-level, who a struggling to serve in those volunteer leader positions.

It was during this time that I really leaned into a specific passion in my heart of building up and developing women as leaders. However, no matter how much I instructed, trained, and encouraged these women, I could not remove the obstacle in their way. Their gender. I could only take them so far. This is one of those moments when I think back to being a child and told: *You can do anything, if you put your mind to it.* Only to realize this was not true. The more women I encountered, the more I realized that this was more than just my issue, or my denomination. In fact, there are more churches that support a stained glass ceiling than those who don't.

Struggling with Limitations

In my research for this book, I reached out to women in leadership across the globe. Those who have successfully navigated the stormy waters, the ones who found sure footing, and those who have tumbled under the weight of the waves. The majority of their stories were grounded in struggle, very few women shared that their path into church leadership was an easy one. Interestingly enough, the women who had the most success were those who lived outside of the United States.

While I had no end of women willing to share with me their experiences, finding even a dozen of them willing to put their name to print was another issue. Much like Virginia Hearn, I faced some obstacles. When Virginia reached out, over forty years ago, the women responded mostly with regret that they couldn't participate. The overwhelming response was out of fear of the repercussions. At this point women were trying, or at least just starting, to make some gains. The women she reached out did not want to rock the boat.

"I am not free to tell..."

"Too painful to relive..."

"Fear the backlash..."

"I am not courageous enough."

"I will be ostracized."

"...will result in doors being shut in my face."

"They will blame this for all faults in my life."

"It would depress you..."

"This would end my chance to ever speak or influence change."

The concerns the women referenced then mirror the same responses I received over forty years later. This is an indication of the lack of stability, women are still fearful of undoing what progress has been made that they are playing the quiet game. Where we tuck our heads down, don't make eye contact, and keep our thoughts to ourselves. Should we speak up or challenge, we could lose what little we have gained. It's a lack of a willingness to risk that compels us into further silence.

When you are already existing with limitations that you feel have been gifted to you, the last thing you want to do is sacrifice those inches in order to fight for the miles. Which leads us to the root of the problem; we are still in a season where women feel like the gains we have made in leadership within the church is a gift... the exception not the norm. Thus it is fragile, and we protect it for our own present gain and as an investment for future women that will come after us. So we bury our talents to protect them.

The responses of the women that turned down Virginia Hearn's request could be categorized as:

- Fear of Being Ostracized

- Fear of Losing Position
- Fear of Recession

The Fear of Being Ostracized includes a concern of being the "only woman in the room" standing against the crowd. By speaking up, or challenging the status quo, you will be in isolation from everyone you are in community with. You may even find yourself in opposition to the members of your own family. This wasn't limited to male community or family members, but also female. What was acceptable in the culture of the time meant that any challenge to the status quo would make everyone uncomfortable. When culture has conditioned women to be quiet, passive, and submissive, it is no surprise that women were more apt to fall silently into the shadows than stand out as a voice in the light.

The Fear of Losing Position was a legitimate concern for those women who had begun to find places of leadership. Whether it be as a volunteer or staff member, when someone starts to draw too much attention, there is a threat to losing their position. Which brings back to attention the earlier point that our advancement is seen as a gift and an exception. Being one of few women at the time to find success, position was absolutely something you could lose. The cost often didn't come at the position itself, but also future positions. The very real fear of everything you worked hard to achieve being not just taken from you, but potentially finding yourself blacklisted from ever serving or leading again, is a threat to the marginalized to stay in line... or else, would be enough to choose silence.

Fear of recession is the weight that all of us carry, when we speak against unfairness or injustice we risk not only personal retribution but also a wake. A wake that will knock down every other woman along with us. We carry this burden, as trailblazers, knowing that if we are not careful it can result in more harm than good. Therefore we measure every step, calculate every word, and intentionally avoid anything that might shift perspective of our abilities.

At the time that I left my previous church of ten years, I was uncertain whether or not the issue was me personally. I hadn't begun investigating the experiences of other women. I thought perhaps I was *too much* for others. That my leadership development had been *too male centric* in the secular world, thus I was leading more like a business man than a Christian woman. I believed that I needed to step more cautiously as a woman in ministry.

As I entered into a new church, the decision had been made that I would tame myself down and not allow my personality to impact how people perceived me. I would keep my head down, thankful for what I was allowed to do. I wouldn't push for more. I was really no more than the aforementioned dog being thankful for bread crumbs in hope that I would eventually get a whole slice. Not even a loaf. Not even a steak. Just a slice.

Despite my best efforts, I could never get beyond the crumbs.

My experiences affirmed that the women of Virginia's time would have been valid in their fears and concerns. As I continued to sift through the conversations with women of my own time, I found that these fears and concerns were just as prevalent today as they were for Virginia... if not more so.

In early 2020, I sat down with an executive team leader from a larger multi campus church. Seeking her advice, as I was growing weary of trying to find a place in ministry and feeling rejected. I cited examples of times where my voice was disregarded; had I been listened to, specific issues could have been avoided. Then, once in crisis, I would be sought out to help create the solution and clean up the mess that I saw coming, and tried to warn against. This is what she said to me:

"Gena, it is sad that we are still in this place, but we must play the game. We can't just tell them [the men], we have to lead them to it so that they believe they came to those ideas themselves. We ask questions that lead their thoughts."

When I suggested that I didn't want to play games, and that it wasn't right in 2020 that we would even need to, she replied:

"You can't just think of yourself. You must consider the women who are coming after you. You may never get what you are looking for, but you are opening the door for her. You need to leave a sweet taste in their mouths."

In a single conversation it became apparent that things hadn't changed that much in forty years. Women are still fearful of being ostracized, losing position, and leaving a black mark that will impact generations of women to come. These are oppressive concepts.

In Aimee Byrd's book *Recovering from Biblical Manhood & Womanhood,* she writes about the early documents related to Complementarian beliefs that suggested that a woman's function is to affirm men's strength and leadership. She references where John Piper wrote, in *Vision of Biblical Complementarity,* that women needed to filter themselves to not affront or threaten men's masculinity, offend their God given authority, and convert God's created order. To which Byrd questioned, *"Is God's created order that delicate, that a man needs to be careful about whether a woman giving him directions is doing it in a personal and directive manner? Do women need to so manipulate their words to be careful not to damage the male psyche if they have something to teach a man?"*

Forty years later, we are still struggling with the same limitations as the women listed among the pages of Hearn's book. Much more seems to be on the line for us now, as I struggled to find women to contribute to this update on her work. While she had a limited access at the time to her own network of contacts, I have the entire world at my finger tips. Yet, I find less women willing to sign their names to the pages. Some even fearful about giving an anonymous account, due to the details potentially revealing who they are or identifying their church.

We are still struggling in part because we are still afraid. How do we begin to address a problem within the church, when the fear outweighs the truth? When those of us who are a part of the culture of the church feel that our value is so loosely held that the slightest strain would cause it to break? A gift that can be stripped from us. What does this say about our church culture when women are afraid to speak up lest they be punished or reprimanded?

First, we must see that our unique talents, passions, skills, and callings are not a gift or an exception. Rather, these parts of us were woven into us at our very creation as we were knit in our mother's wombs. Scripture instructs us that we are part of The Great Commission, part of a body with many parts, and parts that are necessary for the whole body to function. This means that our roles in leading within the church are not confined, not an exception, nor a gift that the few of us should be grateful to receive.

We are called. Commissioned. It is an expectation of us that we are part of the expansion of the Kingdom. We are students sitting at the feet of Jesus, as women's Bible studies outnumber male studies in great disproportion. In 2017, Barna Research revealed that 60% of Christian women read their Bibles for or more times per week, compared to Christian men at 40%. For many years it has been noted that women comprise the greatest number of volunteer roles in the church. The Bureau of Labor Statistics study in 2014 revealed that women volunteer at a rate of 29% higher than men. Yet, women hold the fewest paid staff positions in the church at just barely over 20% (a rise of 2.3% since 1960).

Imagine your church, right now. What would happen if every female volunteer resigned? Would the men step up to fill those holes? Are there even enough men to do so? Could you afford to hire people to fill those abandoned positions? Could your church continue to function on a day to day basis, without the women who have been giving of their time, talent, income, and so much more?

This is a valid concern considering that the statistics are also revealing that women are already leaving the church. Once there was a huge gender gap between the attendance rates of men and women. In any given church, on any given Sunday, 60+% of the attendees were female. That gap has begun to close. Not because male attendance has increased, but due to the mass exodus of women. Overall attendance is down, and women's attendance specifically has dropped by nearly 31% in the last decade, according to Barna Research. The women are leaving. Their gifts and talents leave with them.

Barna Research founder, George Barna, wrote on his website that *"For years, many church leaders understood that 'as goes women, so goes the American church".* He continued, *"Looking at the trends over the past 20 years, and especially those related to the beliefs and behavior of women, you might conclude that things are not going well for conventional Christian churches."* **The findings in Packard & Hope's** *Church Refugees* **research confirms Barna's results. I fear that the disconnection from the local church during Covid19 created the opportunity for even more women to disengage from their churches and quietly slip out the back door. Our post Covid19 statistics will most likely reflect a deeper plunge.**

The driving force behind this exodus is the deep desire to be an active, invested participant in the church versus a consumer. Volunteers and leaders want to be a part of a meaningful work. Packard & Hope found that the *"bulk of the dechurched were extraordinarily active, committed members of their congregations. --- They were the ones showing up early to set up worship spaces, attending planning meetings, implementing group decisions, leading Bible studies and youth groups, organizing retreats and outreach and small groups, and a whole host of behind the scenes things that make churches run and give life to community. --- Most of this energy was poured into the church without compensation. --- They wanted to be active participants in their churches, but only if their participation can be meaningful. This is not to say that the dechurched are unwilling to engage in the mundane, daily tasks necessary to keep a congregation going. Instead, the tipping point comes they feel those are the only tasks they're allowed to do. Internally, they want to be involved in relationship formation and cultivation, and externally, they desire to be missional and impactful in their local communities."* (pg 57)

In real life, this is reflected in the following stories that I observed or were shared with me.

In 2017, at a conference, I overheard a woman sharing that at her church women couldn't lead a Bible Study on their own, expositorily. They were only permitted to facilitate a study, so long as it was written by Beth Moore or Kay Arthur. A second woman shared that she was only permitted to teach from materials written or edited by Kathleen Neilsen. A third shared that she could only purchase study materials for her women's group that were published by Lifeway.

In 2018, a woman told me that she was excited for my book, *Women's Ministry with Purpose,* because for the first time in her church's history a woman was going to lead the women's ministry. The elder who was in charge felt it was time for him to hand it over to a woman.

In 2019, a friend celebrated that for the first time ever in the history of her church, a woman was going to open the service in prayer. In 2018, I was one of the first women in the history of our church to deliver the announcements and open our service in prayer.

In 2020, one of my closest friends shared with me that her pastor had approached her and her husband one day, asking about sharing her testimony in church. Only to arrive on the morning of to find out that it would be her husband that would share her testimony for her. She could stand with him.

In 2021, a woman shared with me that she had been serving faithfully in a volunteer position for over eight years that fell within her field of expertise. When the church decided to hire someone full time for the position, they hired a recent male college graduate that never even set foot in their church.

In 2022, a woman recently hired as a ministry leader shared with me that she was offered 1/5th of the going pay rate for that position in her state. She only accepted it because she was the first woman to ever be offered that position in her church network. She took the offer, no attempt to negotiate, because she felt like it was a big enough move to break the stained glass ceiling. This was progress that she didn't want to derail.

One night, as I was lamenting over the current state of affairs for women serving in the church, my husband said...

"Women are the backbone of the church. If it wasn't for the women the majority of the stuff wouldn't get done. I don't know why you all even allow yourselves to be treated this way."

His words implied that we had a choice.

Hearn indicated they were the emerging leaders.

Forty years later, are we still *just* emerging?

CHAPTER THREE:
STRUGGLING WITH HISTORY

When we examine the historical timeline, it reveals that women carry a strong influence in the early church through to recent history. While this book was not intended to focus on the office of the Pastor, it would be remiss to not include that information as part of the larger scope of women's service in the church. When the historical timeline is taken into consideration, it demonstrates that the struggle for women to serve in the church or in leadership capabilities has not improved since early church days, and more accurately the needle actually may be moving backwards. These backward shifts are most evident in the patristic era (100-500AD), post Industrial Revolution, post World War 1 and 2, and in response to the feminist movements of the late 60s and 70s.

> *"In protestant theology women were not forbidden to be heard according to the universal ministry doctrine "all of us are priests, provided we are Christians "Luther said in 1520. His claim also meant that priesthood was not sacred, "priesthood being just a ministry" (meaning service). "*
> *(museeprotestant.org)*

In some regards, I believe that part of our struggle lies in semantics. Between denominations, traditions, and even historically, we have words with definitions that evolved, injection of new words with similar meanings but different applications, and the general concerns of context. This will be discussed further in chapter six.

Starting our timeline in the Old Testament, it is filled with women that were making decisions, taking stands, and helping advance the Kingdom. Exodus established the priesthood to be exclusive to the sons of Aaron, but priesthood was not the only leadership role available. Consider Deborah the wise judge and prophetess, Esther the Queen who risked all to save her people, The Proverbs 31 Woman who was running a home and business, Jael who had command over that tent peg, or the likes of Rahab who hid the Hebrew spies; women were active participants in the advancement of God's plans.

Let's examine the historical timeline, as well as some of the many firsts in recorded history.

1400 BC - Exodus 40:15 - Establishment of Priesthood (Sons of Aaron, Levites) Miriam, first recorded worship leader and first recorded female prophet (Exodus 15:20)

1107 BC - Deborah, prophet and first recorded female judge of Israel (Judges 4)

Moving forward into the New Testament, the accounts of the disciples and crowds indicate that Jesus' ministry was followed and supported by both men and women. His miracles were performed for men and women alike. He conversed with men and women. He traveled with both men and women. In fact, for the time period, Jesus' relationship with women would be considered radical. He valued women so much, that he traveled out of his way to encounter the Samaritan Woman at the Well; to whom the Scriptures credit her testimony as the reason many in the town were saved.

The New Testament reveals an expansion of leadership beyond the priesthood. Thus creating more opportunity for believers to step into leadership within the Kingdom, whether they were leading just a few as a teacher, leading a house church, or going out on missionary journeys. Where the Old Testament established roles like priest, prophet, and judge, the New Testament introduces patrons, teachers, missionaries, deacons, elders, etc. As Christ brought people under His leadership, we were commanded to step out as ambassadors in His authority to seek the lost and guide them to the Truth. The Scriptures did not exclude women from being commissioned.

33 AD - Matthew 28:16-20 – The Great Commissioning of all Believers Mary, first person to see the risen Christ, and deliver the Good News

55/56 - Paul writes to Deaconess Phoebe (Romans 16)

60/62 - Paul writes to Ephesians regarding various roles people called to (Ephesians 4:11-16)

64/65 - Paul writes to Timothy, regarding the Office of the Overseer (1 Timothy 3)

In the immediate years following Christ's crucifixion, resurrection, and ascension, many of the followers would establish home churches in their towns and others were called out into the mission field. Historical records of the martyrship of Christians include both men and women who paid the price for their convictions and dedication to sharing the Gospel Message. By the time of Paul's letters to Timothy, some resistance to women in leadership roles was emerging. In about 100AD, we entered into the patristic age, where male dominance influenced both church and society for the next several hundred years.

There is some disagreement between the early church shapers, some suggesting that they favored women as equals and tried to bring dignity to women. However, there were many who shared the views of the Greeks and Romans, where men were the dominant and women were the passive gender. Male virility and status was supreme, and at best women as the weaker sex were there to support the males' quest. Scriptures would be used to support this, which we will discuss in more depth in chapter five. This male dominant posture is not unlike what was experienced in more recent history, such as the 1970's feminist movement.

160-220 AD – Tertullian (early Christian author, apologist, and a polemicist against heresy) viewed women as the devil's gateway

423-457 AD – Theodoret of Cyrus (influential theologian of the School of Antioch, biblical commentator, and Christian bishop of Cyrrhus) favored women in leadership roles, insisting that God made woman from man so that they would be essentially in unity with one another, in harmony. He observed that there were some instance where women better handled adversity

347-420 AD – St Jerome viewed women as the root of all evil, and too easily deceived

347-407 AD – John Chrysostom (bishop of Constantinople) viewed women as the weaker sex, stating: *"were great characters, great women and admirable.... Yet did they in no case outstrip the men, but occupied the second rank"* (Epistle to the Ephesians, Homily 13)

Unfortunately due to the scarcity of documents from this age, it is hard to know exactly how much influence women had and in which roles they participated in. It is generally believed that women did, despite the opposition, hold office and influence the growth of Christianity. In the 3rd Century, we do know that women were holding the office of deaconess (Council of Nicaea, Apostolic Constitutions), but this role was limited. Deaconesses would perform duties that were improper for their male counterparts. Another office for women during this time was the Order of Widows, which the exact duties varied depending on the church. In some instances the widows were considered lay leaders but not ordained; others considered it ordained and part of clergy.

The office of Presbyters, was one of contention and where the greatest debate remains to this day. Presbyters are elders or ministers of the church. In the patristic age, various councils attempted to close the office of the Presbyters for women. Due to a lack of documentation, and that the position was seemingly rare, the exact duties of female Presbyters is unknown. A letter from Pope Gelasius does confirm that there were some female Presbyters in the Italian "orthodox" church, as well as a few Latin inscriptions that suggest in parts of Italy there may have been female Bishops.

The Middle Ages, 500-1500, male hierarchy in the church was influencing society and the politics of the day. Attitudes against the ordination of women, and women in general leadership within the church, were making gains. There were still women leading in various capacities, but not without limitations and opposition. This resulted in the rise of Christian Convents where women could advert domesticity and instead increase their theological knowledge and participate in worship on a full time basis. Albeit a lay movement, the women in charge of these convents carried great influence in their communities.

Despite the oppositions women faced in theological advancement from the church itself, their access to the Wycliffe Bible allowed for self-teaching directly from the Word. This was quite upsetting to the male-centric church authorities and even the possession of parts of the Wycliffe Bible could result in execution.

1382/85 – John Wycliffe translates the Bible into English, many women learned to read so they could read the Scriptures for themselves. Women become major distributors of the Wycliffe Bible. Eventually, women (particularly single women) become a major force in Wycliffe translations into other languages

1526 – Women, such as Yolande Bonhomme, were a force in the copying / printing of the entire Bible for distribution

In the 1600s, the Reformation brought in a renewed reverence of the role of wife and mother, so came the approval of women's increased literacy through the reading of the Scriptures. No longer a capital offense, women could freely read the Bible and were encouraged to do so. Martin Luther supported women's literacy for the sake of being steeped in the Word. Luther encouraged his own wife to memorize portions of Scripture.

However, with the Reformation also came a limiting of Protestant women's options for religious roles as the convents were shut down in reformed communities. If not here, then where do the women go? How do they fulfill their calling when those avenues are removed and the church attitude had been steadily growing colder toward women in leadership? This also put limitations on women's formal theological education and training. Even though Luther supported women's literacy and Scripture memorization, he was still among his contemporaries in the belief that a woman's place was in the home. The majority of the Protestant churches held firmly to the cessation and restrictions upon women serving in church leadership, at the beginning of the Reformation period.

Over time, as denominations split or new ones were formed (including independent and non-denominational), the number of exceptions to that stance grew. Approaching the 20th century, a number of churches began to open the doors for women in lead-

ership positions. This included official titles such as Pastor or Deaconess, and extended to Executive and Administrative positions in
the church. As the church complex grew to employ varied positions
that didn't exist in the days of the home churches, so do employment options. At least in theory.

It was during this time, particularly in the American church,
that the number of women attending church began to outnumber
the men. Women were the predominant volunteers that served to
support the day-to-day operations of the church. Often these roles
were similar to the domestic roles they filled at home, translated to
the church. Women were making meals for shut-ins or those hospi-
talized, cleaning the church or performing secretarial duties, playing the organ/piano or leading the choir, and tending to the babies
in the nursery, or teaching in the children's Sunday School classes.
Additionally, women's Bible Study and prayer groups began to outnumber the men's groups. There was also growth in the number
of touring women's conferences and retreats for women to attend,
with the options available to men paling in comparison. Women
were beginning to make strides.

1630/40 - Elizabeth Hooton, 1st woman recognized as a Quaker
    Preacher

George Fox wrote about her death: *"Elizabeth Hooton, a woman
of great age, who had traveled much in Truth's service, and suffered
much for it, departed this life. She was well the day before she died,
and departed in peace, like a lamb, bearing testimony to Truth at her
departure." (quakersintheworld.org)*

1630/70 - Asenath Barzani, 1st recorded female Rabbinical scholar,
    possibly Rabbi

1770 - Mary Evan Thorne, 1st Methodist "Class Leader" (equivalent to lay pastor)

1775 - Anne Lee, founder of Shakers

1755 - Pope Benedict XIV explicitly condemned females serving as priest

"Pope Gelasius in his ninth letter (chap. 26) to the bishops of Lucania condemned the evil practice which had been introduced of women serving the priest at the celebration of Mass. Since this abuse had spread to the Greeks, Innocent IV strictly forbade it in his letter to the bishop of Tusculum: "Women should not dare to serve at the altar; they should be altogether refused this ministry." We too have forbidden this practice in the same words in Our oft-repeated constitution Etsi Pastoralis, sect. 6, no. 21." (On the Observance of Oriental Rites, Pope Bendict XIV – 1755)

Women were expected to be in the home, tending to the children, caring for their husbands. With the the Industrial Revolution, 1780-1840, entering the scene, men were leaving the home and heading to work in factories. The women were left home to care for the children. It was during this time that the responsibility of rearing the children (both practically and spiritually) shifted from both parents to falling squarely on the shoulders of the mother. This was the birth and height of "motherhood being a woman's greatest calling". A phrase that is still prominently argued from pulpits and church circles today.

During the Industrial Revolution there was an increase of Catholic educational and nursing religious institutes. Women had a huge influence in the development and operation of educational and heath care establishments. It was common at this time for single women to find employment as a nurse, school teacher, shopkeep, and other similar jobs; that is until they got married. The cultural expectation of the time would be for a woman to resign upon marriage (preferably) or pregnancy (at latest).

1760/1840 - Industrial Revolution

1819 - Jarena Lee, 1st woman authorized to preach in African Methodist Episcopal Church

1847 - With America's expansion to during the Pioneer Days, women often filled the role of Pastor. Early Pioneer churches did not have much distinction between the sexes on grounds over whom could serve at the altar

1850 - Phoebe Palmer, Methodist Evangelist

"Her theology of the "altar covenant" was influential in the founding of the Church of the Nazarene, The Salvation Army, The Church of God, and The Pentecostal Holiness Church. Her book, The Way of Holiness was in fifty-two editions by 1867." (cbeinternational.org)

1851- Antoinette Brown Blackwell, 1st ordained woman of Congregational Church

1855 - Julia Evelina Smith, 1st woman to translate the Bible into English, self-published

1866 - Margaret Newton Van Cott, 1st woman licensed to preach Methodist Episcopal Church

1869 - Lydia Sexton (United Brethren Church), 1st woman appointed US prison chaplain (KS)

1876 - Anna Oliver, 1st woman to receive a Bachelor of Divinity degree (BUST)

1885 - Maria Woodworth Etter, begins preaching

1884 - Marion Macfarlane, 1st woman to be ordained in the Anglican Church (Australia)

1889- Louisa Woosely, 1st ordained Presbyterian (also 1st Reformed Pastor in America)

Aimee Byrd wrote in her book, *Recovering from Biblical Manhood and Womanhood,* of this time period, *"The culture of the time was steeped in Victorian-era values and ideals of what it means to be a man and a woman. Still replying on ancient Greek assumptions, society maintained that women's brains were considered inferior to men's, incapable of contributing at the same intellectual and social level."* It is this belief system that makes all of these first women so incredibly special for the time period, but also should cause us to consider the implications of that type of thinking still existing today. Our current generations of women are far more educated not just academically, but also theologically and practically.

In 1914, war was on the horizon. We would face two world wars that would take our husbands and sons out of the factories, garages, and offices and onto the battlefield. Women were now overseeing the home, rearing of the children, and standing in the workplace for the enlisted men. Some of these women were relieved when their husband came home safely, and could not wait to be stationed back in their homes. However, a great number of women faced the need for employment because their husband was a casualty of war, or they simply found fulfillment in their employment. Perhaps, they liked the added income or found a renewed sense of value and importance.

When thinking of women filling in for our men off at war, the images that most of us conjure is that of women working in the factories. Our minds instantly envision Rosie Riveter, with her bicep curled to form a muscle and her hair tied up in a handkerchief. However, our churches were not exempt from the cost of war. Women were filling in for pastors. This was acceptable, even to the harshest critics, since it was out of necessity as there were no men available. During this season, women were being ordained in more denominations, and those who were ordained generally continued in their positions after the end of World War II.

1914 - Maria Woodworth Etter was pivotal in founding Assemblies of God

1919 - Agnes White Diffee, 1st ordained Nazarene

1918 - Women serve as "messengers" for the Southern Baptist Convention (SBC)

1920s - Some Baptist denominations begin ordaining women

1924 - Helen Barrett Montgomery, first woman to translate NT for major publisher

1930 - Berthe Bertsch, 1st ordained woman of Protestant Reformed Church

1937 - Geneviève Jonte, 1st ordained woman of Lutheran Evangelical Church

1939/45 - During WWII – women filled in for pastors/priests during the deployments

1947 - Luthern Protestant Church begins ordaining women

1949 - Elisabeth Schmidt, 1st Ordained Woman for Reformed Church of France

1950 - Post WWII, Female Domesticity established, as well as the roots of the concept of Biblical gender roles

1956 - Margaret Ellen Towner, 1st woman ordained in the PCUSA

It was at this juncture, when the men came home to resume their jobs … and the women were not ready to give them up. That friction began to move toward action and activism. In response to the women striking out in independence, there was more pressure put on the women to fall into line with what was deemed acceptable for their gender. Many of the modern stereotypes that are ascribed to femininity, especially biblical femininity are rooted in this 1950s sentimentality. Those women who didn't want to fall in line, who wanted to keep their jobs, the women who wanted higher education, equal opportunities, equal pay, and for those who wanted to serve without limitation in the local church, these women ignited the Women's Movement of the 60s and 70s.

1960 - Rise of Women's Movement

1964 - Addie Davis, 1st Ordained Woman in Southern Baptist Convention

Late 1960s - Societal changes for full equality of women

1970 - Increase of women attending seminaries

In the 1970's, women were being accepted into seminaries for formal theological training. In some instances, this was a move that was still in line with the accepted stereotypical roles for women in the church. I personally know of several women who attended a seminary or bible college pursing a degree in music with the expectation of being the lead organist/pianist or leading the choir. It was a common thought that women attended seminary to get their MRS. degree, in order to land a husband who is called to pastor. This perception can still be found today, often found in lighthearted *jokes* when discussing women in seminary.

As the feminist movement gained more traction, men felt threatened. Not far from the same arguments used in regard to the abolition of slavery, desegregation, and immigration, men voiced fear of losing their jobs to women. To the point of insinuating that women were incapable of doing the same quality of work, if able to do it at all depending on the industry. Some didn't like the idea that a woman didn't need a man. In situations of domestic abuse, these men definitely didn't want women to be able to survive independently. There were women fighting for their rights to more opportunities for employment, and then there were women who were fighting for equal pay to their male counterparts or for equal advancement opportunities.

There was tension, and it made its way into the church. Church leaders from multiple denominations began meeting to address the Church's response to the feminist movement. This resulted in digging their heels into the ground over limiting and outright banning women in church leadership positions, as well as creating an official definition or foundations to what would be called Biblical Manhood and Biblical Womanhood. From here, the term Complementarianism enters the debate against Egalitarianism.

1984 - Women as pastors challenged by Independent Baptists Southern Baptist Convention adopted a resolution opposing women's ordination

1988 - Danvers Statement drafted by Council on Biblical Manhood and Womanhood

1991 - Presbyterian Church of Australia ceased ordaining women to the ministry. *Recovering Biblical Manhood and Womanhood: A Response to Evangelical Feminism* by John Piper and Wayne Grudem is published

2000 - Baptist Faith Message was amended: the office of pastor is limited to men

2010 - 1st time in history of the Church of England, more women than men were ordained

What is key in this timeline is that these challenges against women were predominantly experienced in the United States more so than globally. As women were being restrained in the US, they were still advancing in other countries. Just a few years ago, I was speaking with a woman who born in Jamaica but had lived in various parts of the world. When I began to talk about the struggles of women serving in the church, she looked at me like I was speaking a foreign language. Outside of the United States, she had not seen this same level of difficulty.

In the last twenty years, the debate about women in leadership positions and pastorate may be more volatile and vital that ever before. The invention of the internet, which led to blogging, which led to everyone feeling they had a voice, and ultimately leading to present day social media platforms, has been eye-opening.

Men and women on both sides of the argument of whether or not women can serve as pastors.

Men and women on both sides of the debate on women as elders, deacons, and ministry leadership positions.

The online debates are not kind, very rarely showing the love of Christ to their brothers and sisters, and instead hurling accusations of heresy. The number one, most common phrase in these debates... *"The Bible clearly says..."*

The Bible can not contradict itself. We do need to settle the issue of women in leadership positions once and for all. I wonder, however, if we can ever resolve this issue when women are still struggling to serve in the church in some of the most basic ways?

Why are men threatened by feminism to the point of restricting women so much so that there is a strangulation of their calling and passion? What do Scriptures say and how do we handle those seemingly contradictions? How have we used semantics to create divides and even loopholes in the conversation, so that we can avoid having to confront truth?

Why are we still struggling in these areas, despite our access to information (biblical and extra biblical)?

Where is our Hope?

CHAPTER FOUR:
STRUGGLING WITH FEMINISM

In the 1960's the women's movement was on the rise, and by the 70's feminism was a major cultural shift. Women were no longer accepting what was being gifted to them, the crumbs from the proverbial table. Not only were they not accepting it, they had moved from debating for change to outright demanding it. This created a divide between those who supported progress and those who wanted to maintain the status quo.

Some men (and women) were terrified that the women's liberation movement was going to destroy their way of life, which they were quite comfortable with. There are always people who are resistant to change, regardless if the change is for the better or the worse. We enjoy what is familiar, and anything that challenges that familiarity becomes the enemy. Men were afraid women would take their jobs, were incapable of doing the job altogether, or bucked at the notion that women needed to be anything more than a wife and mother. There was an inability to understand the female desire to exist outside of domesticity. Just as much as there were some women who were content in their domestic roles, who feared being thrust into the workplace in order to add to the familial income.

By this point there was a generation of men who knew no difference than women being in the home. Their fears were affirmed by small groups of women who did have extreme feminist views. History has shown on more than one occasion that every movement (good and bad) always has a radicalized subset, which usually gets the most attention due to their extreme views and aggressive actions. However, the majority of women in the movement were seeking not to surpass men but find equality. These women didn't want to steal the men's seats at the table, but believed there was room at the table for everyone. Plenty of seats, plenty of tables.

The response to the feminist movement was a bearing down on patriarchal ideals. If society could be convinced that the best place for women was in the home, and men in the workplace, their fears would be quelled and life could go on. One way to ensure these ideals were cemented into society was for the church to take an official stance on feminism. Several leaders from the major denominations gathered to discuss how the church would respond to feminism, and through that meeting the concepts of Biblical Manhood and Womanhood would be laid out. These men determined that there was an *equal but different* approach to gender. Men and women were equal in the eyes of the Lord in regards to their value and importance, but different in their role and purpose within Kingdom advancement.

Last year, frustrated with the difficulty I was facing in ministry work, I reached out to a colleague for advice. I was attempting to understand why I couldn't get beyond the obstacles in my way as a women's ministry leader. I could see the potential for so much more, and I felt restrained. I wasn't prepared for her response, in all honesty. Quite taken aback actually, so much so that I'm not even sure that I responded to it. She said, "*Gena, men are threatened by women's theological knowledge. They do not want the women advancing past them in that area. A husband doesn't want his wife to know more of the Bible than he does.*"

Even though more women are attending church then men do.

Even though women's Bible study groups outnumber men's study groups.

Even though women volunteer in church more than men do.

In fact, the only two areas that women are not exceeding the men is in seminary attendance and pastorate (cumulative over all denominations and independent churches). Those numbers are currently growing. Based on her words, I suppose women are to slow down or stop completely until the men catch up. Statistics show that the men are not trying to close the gap, but in fact their attendance numbers and study habits are waning. There is nothing in Scripture that supports the notion that women are to not pursue God and understanding His Word with all their hearts, minds, and understanding. Quite contrary, as we are told to meditate on the Word at all times, in all the things we do. In waking, working, resting.

Motherhood, The Greatest Calling

Those associated with this response would coin the term Complementarian, and began the narrative that domesticity and motherhood is the greatest calling for women (some would argue only). At the time of the writing of this book, this narrative is still being spoken from pulpits, in women's Bible study groups, and in Christian moms' groups or homeschool circles. Motherhood is sacred work, but it isn't our commissioning. If this was our greatest calling, and all that God wants from us (to have children, raise them in the Scriptures), how then do we reckon with women who are childless? Why would God establish something as a mandate only to prevent some women from being able to fulfill it? That seems out of character for the Lord.

I've always questioned whether or not it was biblical and responsible to suggest that motherhood was the highest, greatest, or holiest calling of women. Every time I heard it taught or spoken, it sounded as if the person was trying to present some new idea that we had never considered before. A revelation of our time. In the pages from Virginia Hearn's book, I found this to untrue. In several of the accounts, the contributors referenced this phrase. This was no new idea, no matter how it was repackaged and dished out. An antiquated view that restricts women's spiritual efforts to the confines of their home. Far from the description of the Proverbs 31 woman that is valued and called blessed.

In Genesis, God does proclaim for Adam and Eve to go forth and multiply; there is no argument against. We know through Sarah that God has the ability to open and close a womb at his discretion. Therefore, if motherhood was the highest calling (or only calling) for women, it would make no sense for God to prohibit some women from having the opportunity to yield to that calling. Which is one of the first evidences that while motherhood is a noble calling, it is not everyone's calling. After all, 1st Corinthians 12 unfolds that we are *one* body, made up of *many* parts, and each part has its *own* function or role to play. Just as Ephesians 4 instructs that some are to be pastors, prophets, evangelists, etc., when considering the role of leadership; could we not just as easily consider that some of us are called to be spouses, parents, students, farmers, teachers, etc.?

There is not a single piece of Scripture that indicates or supports that motherhood is a woman's greatest calling. The Scriptures wielded to support that notion merely acknowledge the importance and influence of mothers, but not that it is the highest calling. Proverbs 31 describes a litany of attributes about a woman of noble character. This includes caring for her home, husband, children, being industrious, helping the poor, and other notable characteristics. Yet, in verse 31, we are shown that it is none of these things that earn her praise. It is her fear (*awe, reverence)* of the Lord that is worthy of praise. It is no her womb that grants her husband honor at the city gates, but rather her Godly character.

In Matthew 28, there is no provision that absolves women from The Great Commission. I've not read a single translation that includes an exclusion to women, or that if you are a mother you are absolved of this responsibility. There is no jury duty like exemption, where we can mail the Lord a card asking to be excused because we are currently parenting a child under the age of twelve.

In Marge Mowczeko's piece, *Is Motherhood the Highest Calling for Women*, she writes: "*Jesus did not think that motherhood was necessarily the highest calling for women. He never encourages motherhood when talking with Mary and Martha of Bethany, Mary Magdalene, the Syrophenician woman, the Samaritan woman, or any other woman. And, he doesn't encourage motherhood in his general teaching.*" She goes on to point out that in Luke 11:27, when a woman in the crowd shouts out a blessing over Jesus' mother, that Jesus' response was that the blessed are those who are hearing the word of God and obeying it.

Being a mother is an amazing thing. My heart breaks for the women who desperately desire motherhood and have been denied it. To say that motherhood is not our highest calling does not give permission for a mother to neglect her children or role as a mother. We are to be good stewards of *all* that we have been given, which includes our children. In my many years of women's ministry leadership, I have heard the cries of women who feel somehow broken or less than because they can not do the very thing they have been told their body is designed and destined for. In labeling motherhood as a calling for all women, or the greatest calling, an enormous amount of unfair pressure is laid upon their shoulders. Not to mention the pain inflicted upon their hearts.

When a woman gets married, she is quickly questioned about when she will start a family. Pregnant women are questioned if they will continue to work once their babies are born. There is a lot of pressure in the evangelical milieu for women to stay home with the children versus returning to work, even more so in the ultra conservative or fundamental sects. This is not much different from the expectations of prior decades where women could work (in specific fields) where upon marriage or pregnancy they would resign to the homestead.

In the modern church, single women often feel overlooked in ministry. As if they have nothing to offer since they lack the sage wisdom that comes with marriage or motherhood. Despite their own significant experience, education, knowledge, talents, and other offerings. We do a disservice to single women by diminishing their worth due to the lack of a wedding band or gaggle of children underfoot. Nor, does the mere title of wife or mother automatically gift a woman with godly wisdom.

Women are Second Class Citizens

Throughout history and even in some modern-day cultures, women are viewed as less than. Second-class citizens with few or no rights, their voices silenced, opinions discarded, and they live under a yoke of oppression. Even within the most progressive countries, we can still see remnants of this belief system. It might be most evident in situations that include domestic violence and abuse, exercised in workplaces where women are given menial positions, or specific cultural ideologies. It also hides in plain sight, in what appears to be innocuous ways, within the minutia that builds over time, slowly seeping in.

There are subtle ways in which this subclass structure can go unrecognized. Whenever a women has to work harder than a man to prove her worth, or when she must slowly enter into leadership as to not upset anyone, we are suggesting that she is less than. Less than he is. Less capable. Less trustworthy. Less responsible. Less experienced. Kara M. Angus posted on Twitter, *"Women will quietly serve in a church for years and be denied ministry opportunities that they are called to and gifted for... and a man will come in to the same church and be on a leadership committee and running the men's ministry within 6 months."*

Women also experience this attitude of being less than as they are painted scapegoats for when things go wrong. When a company is dramatically failing, it is a common practice to appoint a new CEO that is female. Studies revealed that this becomes a win/win for the company; should the company continue to fail, they can blame her and if it succeeds, they are seen as progressive. (Investopedia.com, Glass Cliff by Julia Kagan).

The idea of the Glass Cliff isn't really new, we see this in Genesis when Adam blames Eve for his consuming the fruit. She was his scapegoat. When a man falls in ministry, he owns up to his failures, receives some sort of counseling, and can prove his way back into leadership. The ministry continues in his absence, and he may even return to the helm after a season. If a woman falls in ministry, even when she acknowledges her err, the ministry is often shut down and she is not given a chance to redeem herself.

Her fall is blamed on the conventions that Complementarians or those who refuse to let women lead (in any capacity) will use to defend their position. The overall implication that women are the weaker sex (easily manipulated) and untrustworthy (she will tempt him). Who would want a weak, unworthy, temptress in a leadership position or with any authority? There is a fear that she will (intentionally or in her naivety) corrupt him (or the ministry), Oh Jezebel! She is cast down as less than, given limitations on her influence, and distrusted. Women, blamed for all the ills of the world. After all, the fall is all her fault.

Even though Adam ate of his own accord, knowing the rule given to him directly by God.

Just as Ahab was noted as already corrupted, before Jezebel even entered his life.

Is there anything worse than being considered a second-class citizen? Perhaps, feeling completely invisible, or ostracized for not fitting the standards of the day. Several years ago, I was sitting at a conference with a friend whom I believe is an amazing speaker. She commented how overlooked she felt in ministry, that she was invisible, because she didn't look the part. She sighed, with a tear forming in her eye, "*It's like they can't even see me.*"

Married women in Hearn's day experienced, and still felt today, is the melding of the woman's identity into her marriage, into her husband. He is the guy at the gate, getting all the praises, for what she has done or paved the way for him to do, while she sits home making garments and buying vineyards (Proverbs 31). Her role in the marriage is to serve him, because another tenent of Complementarianism is the misapplication of Biblical submission. For too many years the woman's feelings, identity, and rights have been cast aside as less important.

Women are told to be compliant. To not abstain from sex. Not to be pushy or nag. Told not to be controlling. To dress for his gaze. Submission (when not mutual) is oppression. Biblical submission is mutual. She submits to him, and he submits to her (Ephesians 5:21). Society, however, not just within the church, sells a different story.

Advertisements for many decades have centered on how to dress to please your husband, products to use to make your appearance younger, and products that would help a woman curb her appetite or change her personality. Let's not forget, however, that is some of these exact things that become the accusation against her when a woman is assaulted. The rapist will blame her dress, she didn't fight back, she didn't say no, etc. Women have gotten mixed signals on how to attract the man and then equally blamed for his inability to control himself once attracted. As a result, more controls were put over women (oppression) as the modesty movement placed the burden of responsibility on the women and they were expected to submit (even if not practical). Women became prey. Then they became the threat.

The Billy Graham rule was instituted to keep men from finding themselves in compromising positions with women, lest they be accused. Men should not be alone in a room or car, or even in a crowded restaurant table with another woman. I once heard a pastor state that if he came along one of his parishioners stranded on the side of the road in the rain, he would not give her a ride but he would wait with her until assistance came. After finishing up a meeting with my pastor about an event, we agreed to head over to our storage unit to inventory our supplies. It was literally just around the corner, he insisted we take two cars. So much of the attitudes that prevent women from serving to their fullest are based in nothing more than fear. Fear suppresses and oppresses.

When someone is dictating what you can do with your time, how much money you can make, what types of jobs you can hold, how much education you can obtain, how you dress and present yourself, and so on... you become a person who does not have full equal rights. All of this has contributed to women being viewed as less than, second-class citizens. It is no wonder that women were fed up to the point to start the women's liberation movements, and mind boggling that we are still struggling for true equality today. For someone who is supposed to be so fragile, weak, incapable, and ill-suited for leadership, there appears to be an awful lot of fear about her.

Struggling with Gender Roles

The fear men have in regards to feminism is rooted in their desire to have power, position, and priority. Which has been cultivated in them as a birthright for generations. It's an assumption that to make space for women means that they will need to sacrifice. The key misunderstanding in this comes down the matter of qualification. No woman is asking for a job, position, or title because of her gender. She's not demanding the job. What is being asked is to have a fair shot and consideration based on her qualifications. She is asking to be seen as more than just a wife or mother, but a human being... made in the image of God... who has value to contribute to society beyond her womb and serving in the church nursery.

There are women who shun the idea of stepping out of the Biblical Womanhood ideals and speak out against feminism. These are women who are either comfortable in their role, or do feel deeply called to be a wife and mother. They don't see the fuss, and can't wrap their heads around why a woman would want more. My mother told me that when she was growing up, the only thing she wanted was to be a wife and mother. Her life plan was to be a stay at home mom, and then eventually a housewife once the nest was emptied. If you are presently in what you feel genuinely is your purpose, in this case motherhood, it is impossible to understand the convictions of those unlike yourself.

In *Our Struggle to Serve,* one of the women shared that early in her life she embraced these gender roles wholly. She was happy to be a wife and mom, cleaning the home, running errands, and making dinner for her family. One day, she felt a shift of conviction. She realized that she embraced these roles because they absolved her of any responsibility or accountability. The Great Commission was her husband's responsibility, not hers. She was doing her duty at home. Once this conviction got ahold of her, it was hard to shrug off. She realized that she was resigning from her commissioning, and putting all of the burden on her husband which was unfair to him. She also was cutting herself off from the blessing and beauty of being an active participant.

The ideals of what we have applied to women, marriage, and motherhood are not even necessarily Biblical. The Proverbs 31 woman, which is the most quoted piece of Scripture in regards to how women should exist, should be the Biblical model of womanhood. She was a good wife and mother, yes. However, she was also much more than that. The Proverbs 31 woman created products, which she sold in the market, and from those profits she bought land. Up early making preparations for her household, staying up late because she is busy with her tasks. She manages her home, servants, and children making sure their needs are met. Involved in her community, she cared for those who were poor in Spirit, and spoke with wisdom and instruction.

This is not a quiet, meek woman, lost in domesticity. She was strong, smart, industrious, and trustworthy.

Yet, the standard was set by 1950's domestic chores and advertisements on beauty. The philosophy of Christian womanhood was centered on marriage, submission, motherhood, and housekeeping. Scripture was warped and twisted to reinforce these ideals, taken out of context to fit the desired outcome. If read at the superficial level, and out of context, it may seem like the Bible is clear about women's roles. We can not truly understand the Biblical stance on women without considering it from the point of view of the world at the time in which they were given. Context matters. History matters. There are no pink parts of Scripture relegated to women, and blue relegated to men.

There have been levels of inconsistency and hypocrisy when it comes to how women and their contributions are perceived throughout their lifespan. As children, girls who excel in sports or academics are heralded with pride. Upon entering adulthood the conversation shifts to marriage, children. There is a societal stereotype that suggests that women who are independent, competent, competitive, and intellectual are inconsistent with femininity. Consider how smart women or athletic women are portrayed on television and in movies. Women and men who share similar characteristics are labeled differently based on gender. Women are seen as aggressive, men ambitious. Women are bossy, men are leaders. Men are told they can have it all, where women are told we have to choose. As if it is impossible for a woman to be successful in her career, while managing her home, and loving her family well.

The Proverbs 31 woman suggests otherwise.

The missionary couples of the New Testament suggest otherwise, as well.

In *Recovering from Biblical Manhood & Womanhood,* author Aimee Byrd asserts that morality can be culturally constructed, stating that *"Without even realizing it, we can pick up traditions from secular society".* She goes on to say, *"While we are collectively separating men and women in the church in some stereotypical and unnecessary ways. --- We will see that the troubling teaching of biblical manhood and womanhood has thrived under popular Biblicist interpretative methods. Biblicist interpretive methods ironically flourish in our individualistic culture that works against the values of family and community that the biblical manhood and womanhood is trying* to uphold. --- *We do not read God's word alone; we read it within our interpretive covenant communities.*" In other words, our beliefs are not just merely what we have picked out of Scripture on our own, but they are heavily influenced by the culture and traditions of our churches and the leadership we sit under.

The solution Byrd offers is to "*peel back the gender tropes of manhood and womanhood that have been imposed on the church, to reveal a household of brothers and sisters in Christ.*"

Evangelical Feminism

In response to church leaders creating the Danvers Statement, and similar documents that formed the ideals of Biblical manhood and womanhood, evangelical feminism stood in stark opposition and affirmed the equality of women. Those who wrote in support of it felt compelled to do so because of their commitment to Christ. Through their writings, Christ, who was radical for the time period for his view and interactions with women, was the shining star of their argument. Jesus would talk with women about the Scriptures. He traveled with women. He allowed women to publicly touch him. This was culturally unacceptable at the time.

Jesus liberated women. God broke the barrier between male and female through Jesus.

When women of Virginia Hearn's age realized they could be both career and family-minded, educated and teaching others, leading in the fullness of their calling it actually made the domestic parts of their lives not just more tolerable but enjoyable. There was the epiphany that role sharing was not role reversing, but rather each of the individuals excelling in their own strengths. Contributor Joyce Gladwell welcomed that she "*could value menial tasks, after accepting that domesticity was not my sole, or primary role and put that conviction into practice.*" *(Our Struggle to Serve, pg 43)*

Women understood that marriage and children were indeed a blessing but not a calling, a least not an all encompassing one.

They began to experience freedom, out from under the expectation of marriage and children, and find fulfillment and wholeness as a woman of God. Fear was forcing the choice to marry, conform to society. Women could choose to not marry, marry later, not have children, have children later in life. To do so was not rejecting her femininity, but embracing herself the way that God made her and following the path He laid out for her versus the expectations of society.

The women spoke up. Wrote letters, essays, and articles. Women wrote to be heard, to be known, by those who normally wouldn't take the time to listen. Women created support groups and clubs, including the provision of childcare so that all could fully participate. The modern-day moms' group or women's ministry, in your local church, is a descendant of this model.

There was a high price to be paid for those women who stepped into this "rebellion".

A price we are still struggling to pay.

CHAPTER FIVE:
STRUGGLING WITH SCRIPTURE

If you are on Facebook, and in particular follow anyone that has a more progressive view of women in the church, you are going to encounter regular debates about the role of women in the home and church. There are accounts that are run by both men and women that are ultra conservative all the way to the other end of the spectrum, ultra liberal. The die hard Complementarian against the staunchest Egalitarian. On Twitter they seem to follow each other, looking for the fight. On Facebook, you are most likely to encounter these debates within the comment sections of articles posted from a Christian magazines, Christian media, or Christian celebrity author/speakers.

It won't take long to find the accounts that hail motherhood as a woman's greatest calling, or suggest that the way to a happy marriage is total submission. Women being admonished to domesticity: wife, mother, keeper of the home. Just wait for someone with at least 1,000 followers to tweet a quote from Beth Moore, Priscilla Shirer, or Lysa TerKeurst; like a river, the accusations of heresy come flooding in the replies. In my own early days on Twitter, one evening before bed I made a post in support of women's ministry (as in brunches with speakers, Bible study with women, etc.) and by morning I was already being accosted by a man, heralded a teacher of blasphemy, and other lovely spurts of venom toward my character. I hadn't even made a comment about women in leadership, or in pastoral roles. Just about a good old-fashioned women's ministry.

On the flip side, should you make any sort of comment or tweet that indicates you agree with limiting the roles of women, to any degree, be prepared to receive your own dose of venom. You are equally unliked. You are equally disapproved. Instead of being a heretic, you are called oppressive at best and stupid at worst. There is very little tolerance for those who are in the middle, believing that there is truth somewhere between the extremes, or simply still seeking the answers for yourself. Each side wants you to take a *for or against* stand based on **their** beliefs and the information **they** provide. They consider their scripture defenses stronger than the other, or accuse the other party of irresponsible interpretation. This *modus operandi* is identical regardless of what position you subscribe.

It is no wonder that women (and men) do not want to engage in the argument or debate. Quietly seeking answers for themselves and never willing to broadcast what decision they have come to. For some, it is simply a nonissue. If you are attending a church, where you are currently happy with your pastoral appointment, what does it matter if other churches see things differently. The choice is easier to be a peacemaker by avoiding the quarrels about the law, and doing our best to live in peace with everyone. Politics and religion make bad bedfellows, or are impolite guests at the dinner table, as the old cliches go. Best to avoid.

Something that has always stood out to me in any sort of rigorous religious debate is the phrase... "*the Bible is clear about...*". I can not think of an single instance where someone used that phrase in a debate about something that the Bible **is** actually clear about. The Bible is clear that murder is wrong, no one disagrees. The Bible is clear that adultery is wrong, again non-debatable. The phrase is not ever coupled with those topics, because no one would argue that the Bible is *not clear* on those issues.

Yet, when you get into the controversial subjects where the Bible is actually **not** clear, where two or more verses appear to contradict one another, suddenly that phrase becomes the precursor to their perspective; such as in the case of *"the Bible is clear about women preaching"*. Or when *"the Bible clearly says that the women is not to be in authority over man"*. This is what we see suggested in the debates, from both sides. This argument is not new, it's the same tactic used during various human rights debates from the ending of slavery, women's rights, marriage rights, etc. Verses plucked out of the Scripture, taken out of context, and used to justify one's point of view. The adding of *"clearly"* implies that if you perceive things any differently that it is due to your lack of intelligence or ability to understand the Scriptures. Clearly. Indeed.

It was years ago, more than I can count, where I sat under an amazing teacher. She taught me that Scripture needed to be read with 20/20 vision. Twenty verses before, and twenty verses after. The premise of her teaching was that it was irresponsible to just pluck out a verse to wield without considering the context. By reading the twenty verses prior and the twenty verses following, a better understanding, or comprehension, of the verse would be more evident. As the years progressed, and I sat under more sage teachers, my appreciation of the application context expanded.

Reading a selection of Scripture responsibly requires weighing that verse against the chapter in which it is found, the book within which it is recorded, and how it falls within the overarching narrative of the Scripture as a whole. Context also requires understanding the history and culture at the time it was written, the literary style in which it was written, who wrote it, and whom it was written for. We recognize that words have changed meaning over the decades, and it is important to read the text using the definitions of the time in which it was written versus our modern vernacular.

If we truly want to understand what the Scripture supposedly *clearly* states, we must commit to reading and studying these verses under the responsibility to cast aside our own personal beliefs, taught traditions, and applying context into our interpretation process.

So, what does the Scripture *clearly* say about women in leadership?

In my research for this book, I found that there were three main arguments about why women shouldn't be in leadership within Virginia Hearn's original book. These arguments are still prevalent, published in books throughout history and presently in various media platforms. Equally dispersed between women in the pastoral positions and whatever other leadership position that particular person (or denomination) was in opposition to. The first argument contends that women can not be in leadership positions because quite simply we are intellectually the weaker sex. The second proposes that women can not hold leadership positions due to our submission under male authority. The third suggests the notion that women frankly can not be trusted and will corrupt the church/ministry.

It is also worthy to note that the perceived restrictions on women in leadership are not just confined to the church. There are those who believe that these restrictions include being a theological teacher in a university or seminary, as well as within the public sphere including political offices. For the purpose of this book, the main focus will remain on theologically related offices and positions.

Struggling as the Weaker Sex

The idea that women are the weaker sex is an age-old argument. The general consensus being that Eve was mentally weak and unable to not fall prey to the serpent's trickery when he questioned her about eating the forbidden fruit. Thus, how could Eve possibly withstand the ploys of the enemy as a leader of people? The fact that she is specifically called out in 2 Corinthians 11:3 appears to justify a fault laid upon her that was not given to Adam.

*"But I am afraid that just as Eve was deceived by the
serpent's cunning, your minds may somehow be led astray
from your sincere and pure devotion to Christ."*
2 Corinthians 11:3

To further bolster their argument, they refer to the most common piece of Scripture used to refute women in leadership, 1 Timothy 2:11-14, which also lays blame on Eve. Giving Adam precedence as the first created and flat out suggests that it was only Eve that was deceived and not Adam.

*"A woman should learn in quietness and full submission.
I do not permit a woman to teach or to assume authority
over a man; she must be quiet. For Adam was formed first,
then Eve. And Adam was not the one deceived; it was the
woman who was deceived and became a sinner. "*
1 Timothy 2:11-14

This coupling of her being easily deceived, thus weaker, and his position as first created, leads to the second argument.

Struggling as the Submissive Sex

Ephesians 5 is utilized to establish hierarchy, that the man is the head of the wife just as Christ is the head of the church. The argument is that the parallel suggests that if men are to Christ, what women are to the church, then the obvious result is that the men lead women like Christ leads the church. The church does not lead Christ, and thus women can not lead men.

*"For the husband is the head of the wife
even as Christ is the head of the church, his body,
and is himself its Savior."*
Ephesians 5:23 ESV

Women are being told in Ephesians to be submissive to their husbands, and that is corroborated by 1 Corinthians instruction to keep silent in the church, remain in submission, and to get their questions answered by their husbands. Women are put in check. To know their place. Which is not leadership.

> *"The women should keep silent in the churches.*
> *For they are not permitted to speak, but should be in*
> *submission, as the Law also says. If there is anything they*
> *desire to learn, let them ask their husbands at home. For it*
> *is shameful for a woman to speak in church."*
> 1 Cor 14:34-35

1 Timothy also suggests full submission. It seems as if the case is super clear, at least at the superficial level. The argument of women being the weaker sex appears to tow the line of why women should submit. It puts into question not only if we can be responsible with the Word (because Eve was not) but also our capabilities in general.

When a woman pushes against this directive, she is called a troublemaker and named a Jezebel.

Struggling as the Jezebel Spirit

It is important to state, at this point, that there are women who have an agenda that damages the church. Just as much as there are men who do as well. A person set out to harm the church is never gender specific, and both can be equally harmful and devastating. That is something that church members should pray for discernment over, to identify and rebuke such wolves in the clothing of sheep. However, that is not what is being addressed in this chapter.

In the research, which included surveys and interviews with women in leadership, far too many women had a personal encounter with this woman called Jezebel. We first read of her in the Old

Testament, where we meet the wife of Ahab, learn of her wickedness, as she plotted and interfered. Her taking matters into her own hands brings down the judgment of the Lord.

> *"But, there was none like unto Ahab which did sell himself to work wickedness in the sight of the Lord, whom Jezebel his wife stirred up."*
> *1 Kings 21:25*

In the New Testament, we meet another Jezebel in the book of Revelation. A false prophetess who encourages God's followers into sin. While not the same exact woman of the Old Testament, she shares similar characteristics.

> *But I have this against you, that you tolerate that woman Jezebel, who calls herself a prophetess and is teaching and seducing my servants to practice sexual immorality and to eat food sacrificed to idols.*
> *Revelation 2:20*

When the two become intertwined, it further supports the idea that women are untrustworthy, irresponsible, and should be submitting vs. leading : suggesting that they are not capable of leading appropriately due to being easily deceived and overtaken by evil. There is no in-depth interpretation for these scriptures, when they are taken at face value. The question arises then, if the Scripture so clearly states these things about women... why is there such an ongoing debate?

The debate arises due to other parts of the Scriptures that appear to contradict these points, supporting a different point of view. That women are strong, wise, capable, and highly favored members of God's family.

Struggling with Contradictions

To imply that women are the weaker sex and can not be trusted with the Word doesn't align with Scripture where women **were** trusted with the messages of Jesus. When encountering the Samaritan woman at the well, it was through her testimony that the Scriptures account many being saved (John 4:39). It was the women at his empty tomb that were charged with sharing the good news of the resurrected Christ (John 20:17-18). Women were considered by Paul as co-laborers in the mission field, as well as his acknowledgment of their contributions to the emerging church. In the Old Testament women were prophetesses who were entrusted with delivering the direct message or instructions from the Lord himself. If she can be trusted as a prophetess, why would she be mistrusted as a teacher?

Even if we were to exclude the position of Pastor, women were definitely working in the ministry beyond childcare and hospitality. In fact, in the story of Mary and Martha the one who was elevated as doing the most important thing in the moment was Mary (sat at the feet of Jesus) versus Martha (overseeing hospitality). If a woman could not be trusted to responsibly handle the Word of the Lord, what would be the value in emphasizing the ideal of her being a student? This is radical teaching for the time, that women were seen by Jesus to have the mental capacity to understand the Scriptures went entirely against the cultural beliefs of the day.

Kadi Cole, author of Developing Females, once stated in a leadership training that we are currently the most educated generation of women in terms of secular and theological knowledge. Women have been allowed and encouraged to read the Scriptures and receive formal theological education. They are well equipped, yet when they enter into church service they are relegated to domestic duties.

I have taken several versions of spiritual gifts testings, and not once was there a question where I identified my gender. Yet, it is my very gender that excludes me from serving in particular capacities. Which makes no sense at all. Author Lisa Colón DeLay states "I'm not convinced women should bother participating when conservative pastors encourage everyone to take spiritual gifts tests when they are set on giving ministry roles out based on sex/gender and not on gifting." What is the point of testing people in order to reveal their gifts and talents only to dismiss their service based on gender?

This is a direct result of Jesus' willingness to impart Wisdom to the women he encountered and welcomed into his circle. This has made the question of intellectual ability and capability moot. Women not only can interpret and understand the Scriptures, they are excelling at doing so due to their formal education. Women are attending seminary or seeking Biblical certifications at a increasing rates, writing books that extend beyond kitsch devotions or topical Bible studies, and have been an integral part of Bible translating. As the women are increasing their formal education, they are returning on that investment as they teach expository studies in their churches, write academic books, and teach at the seminary level. Women sat as students and thus were equipped to then teach others from what they learned.

Historically, there may have been some legitimacy to the concerns on women being the weaker intellectual sex. That was legitimized, not by their inability but rather by the lack of education available to women; even as it became available it certainly was not encouraged. Women have also risen in the ranks of politics and corporations to establish that their skill sets are not just a value to the home but within the marketplace. No longer are women weaker, the argument falls flat today. It is for this exact reason that context matters. These words are far less contradictory when seen in the light of the culture and time that they were written. Today's women are not the same, nor is the culture. Even John Piper, a hard-line Complementarian, has expressed that the issue has nothing to do with a woman's ability or capability to teach. He argues that it's not a matter of whether they could teach/preach but rather if they should.

In the examination of the argument regarding submission and position, once again we find apparent contradictions. One side argues the women submit based on the aforementioned scriptures, but the other side counters with an equally strong position beyond Galatians 3:28 that suggests we are equal heirs to the Kingdom (no Greek nor Jew, male nor female, slave nor master). The most obvious is to complete the Ephesians 5:23 statement on submission through contextual evaluation. This particular section of Scripture begins at 5:21 which says:

> *"Submit to one another out of reverence for Christ."*

1 Peter 5:5 instructs for the young to submit to the elder for teaching, and for there to be humility between us. In Ephesians, the letter addresses sisters and brothers not just husbands and wives. Submission is rooted in asserting that there is someone in a greater position and someone in a lower, someone who controls the power and someone who is ruled under it. When man fell, God says that the woman will be ruled by her husband. Which means that this concept of created order is not the issue at all, but instead it is a consequence of the fall versus the natural order He intended.

When we examine the creation of Eve, the Bible reveals the very first time in the creation story that God found something *not good*. In Genesis 2:18, the Lord states that it was not good for man to be alone. His solution was the creation of woman, whom he assigned to be Adam's "helper". However the word used here is *ezer*, which is also used to describe God. We wouldn't dare suggest that *ezer* is to be submissive to man, knowing that ezer includes God. That would be blasphemous to place man over God. Therefore, we can not use that term to describe woman and at the same time place man over her in authority. In the creation of man and woman, it is said in Genesis 1:26-28 that they were both made in the image of God, and with the intention of equal dominion over the land.

*"Then God said, "Let us make mankind in **our image**,
in our likeness, so that **they may rule** over the fish in the
sea and the birds in the sky, over the livestock and all the
wild animals, and over all the creatures that move along
the ground." So God created mankind **in his own image**,
in the image of God he created them; **male and female** he
created them. God blessed them and said to them,
"Be fruitful and increase in number; fill the earth
and **subdue it**."*

The Triune God can not have one part that holds dominion over the others. God the Father, the Son, and the Holy Spirit are unified, equal, maintaining the same divine attributes and nature. Each part of the Trinity has a level of mutual submission based on how it works within the unfolding of the larger story. God creates. Jesus saves. Holy Spirit leads. This might seem as an affirmation to the Complementarian posture of "equal but different", in which indicates that while both are equally valued in worth to God, men and women are different in their respective roles.

However, when we are discussing leadership what we are really discussing is authority. In Matthew 28:18, Jesus declares that he has all authority under heaven and on earth. This means that in the matter of authority God the Father, the Son, and Holy Spirit are equal. Man and woman, made in the image of God, are also equal in authority. They have been assigned the same job, to take dominion over the creatures of the world. Eve was not positioned under Adam, but with him. The job was corrupted, but not by a Jezebel spirit in Eve but rather a cunning enemy is who talented at twisting the Word of God.

In Genesis 3, the serpent twists the instructions of God in order to confuse the woman. What is never revealed in Scripture directly is why she was so easily tricked. There is no record that the Lord spoke the command directly to Eve, only to Adam. There are only two possible options: the Lord shared this directive to not eat of the tree with Eve or that Adam, himself, passed that instruction on to her. If it was the Lord, then Eve misunderstood. If Adam dispensed the mandate to Eve, then we are left to question whether or not he passed on those instructions accurately. None the less, these are merely suppositions, that are left unaddressed and unanswered.

What we do know, from Scripture, is that in the moment of Eve's temptation she was not alone. Adam was present (Genesis 3:6). This indicates that he had the ability to stop Eve or decline his own participation, which he chose in his own free will to eat of the fruit. When confronted by the Lord, Adam does not own up to his actions but rather passes the blame to Eve, and eventually to God for creating Eve (Genesis 3:12). Whereas Eve immediately takes responsibility for her action. To take into account the actions surrounding the fall, and to only cast Eve as the weaker sex, the irresponsible one, the person most easily tempted, is a mishandling of the text.

Both bore the responsibility for disobeying the Lord's command to not eat from the tree. One owned up to it, where the other tried to transfer the blame. How could we hold Eve, and thus all women, responsible and barred from leadership when Adam was equally complicit? The creation established man and woman as a pair, charged with overseeing the world, and their temptation corrupted the assignment ultimately leading to consequences. The evidence lay on both their heads. Whilst some might argue that Eve tempted or manipulated Adam into partaking, there is no Biblical evidence to support that argument. Even if there was, one could equally argue that Adam (and thus men) are equally susceptible to deception.

We then consider the final argument, that women are Jezebel spirits trying to usurp authority and cause trouble. In the two depictions of Jezebel, in the preceding scriptures, we encounter two very different women, part of two very different stories. In the first, we have Jezebel who was married to Ahab. This position suggests that Jezebel incited her husband's evil ways (1 Kings

21:25) and is therefore responsible for his corruption. When read in context, this falls short due to the fact that Ahab was already corrupted before Jezebel appears. In fact, it was his corruption that paved the way for Jezebel to become his wife (1 Kings 16:30). His preexisting corruption opened the door for her exploitation. Had he been dedicated and good in the eyes of the Lord, Jezebel would have had no foothold.

Context indicates that the Jezebel of Revelation is not the Jezebel of 1 Kings, no matter how closely they resemble each other. Ecclesiastes reminds us that there is nothing new under the sun. It is of no surprise that there are other women in the course of time that are like the Old Testament Jezebel. This does not discount the sheer number of Godly women who step firmly into the roles the Lord has called them to. Deborahs who judge and lead, Jaels that drive a tent peg in the head of the enemy, Phoebes that serve as Deaconesses, and Joannas that finance the church. To dismiss their gifts and talents, their leadership and wisdom, due to a few Jezebels is frankly a crime against our imago dei. It asks us to bear the wages of sin, to this day, which Christ died for.

Being male does not automatically make you a wise and uncorruptable leader, just as much as being female does not automatically determine that you are not capable of leading well and with proper authority. Headlines have illuminated a myriad of modern day Ahabs, corrupt male leaders in the church. Some of the most notable will offer up an excuse, apologize, take some time off to reflect or enter into therapy, only to resume leadership in a short period of time after. In some instances within the same church, in other instances as apart of a new congregation. We've even witnessed this happen on repeat, where the man is given multiple opportunities to repent and find himself restored to ministry leadership. This same grace is not afforded to women. A woman makes a singular error, and her entire ministry is shut down. Not only that, but she serves as the evidence against other women ever even getting the opportunity to lead.

Instead of being free to fulfill the Great Commission in the way that we have been equipped and called, we are still bound under the penalty of the fall. We dismiss the promises of the Lord made to both his male and female children; leads us to a place of oppression and hypocrisy instead of the freedom we are to find in Christ. How can men be considered qualified and women are denounced when both equally participated out of their own free will in the events of the fall? There is either penalty for both, or freedom for both. God's mercy, goodness, and grace can not have it any other way.

Struggling with that Letter to Timothy

The absolute firework finale in the debate of women in leadership is 1 Timothy 2:12, where Paul writes to Timothy in Ephesus that he does not permit women to teach or assume (or usurp) authority over men. It's the one piece of Scripture that *appears* to be pretty black and white, without any confusion. At the surface level, this would appear to be true. Context calls us to deeper examination. If Paul is apparently putting his foot down against women in leadership here, then within his many other letters he begins to contradict himself.

There are three very specific points to address in this sentence. First, Paul is writing to Timothy about the church in Ephesus. Second, Paul's words about not allowing a woman to teach men contradicts other stances found in Scripture (including within Paul's own words). Third, the language of assuming or usurping authority is key to understanding the implications.

The church in Ephesus was emerging in a city that had a strong pagan history, where women were the chief priestesses. In the conversion of the city, the women would have assumed that they would have the same or similar roles within this new faith budding among their community. In any circumstance, historical or modern, people who have power, position, or influence are rarely interested in relinquishing due to changes in social order or culture. Context clues in the letter help us arrive at sound reasoning behind Paul's apprehension for allowing women to teach in Ephesus. If we do not hold firmly to one verse, but take into consideration the full context of his letter, we see that Paul points out to Timothy that the women of the town were busy going from house to house speaking about things they do not know. This was not mere gossiping, but rather incorrect teaching. Which would explain why Paul's suggestion is for the women to become students, learning in quiet submission to the Lord.

Paul's other letters include references to women whom he considered co-laborers in the faith, accounts of Priscilla and her husband teaching a man (noting that Priscilla's name is mentioned first, and is a possible indicator that she was the primary teacher, as this was not the naming order custom of the time), and the women who Paul considered trustworthy in overseeing their home churches (Phoebe). Just to name a few. Paul could not allow women to teach in other cities, in the mission field, Et al at the very same time as he banned all women from teaching in his letter to Timothy in Ephesus. This was a specific letter, to a specific church, about specific women, and for a specific time. These letters are just as applicable today to cities like Ephesus, reminding us to be students before we take on the role of teacher. Not all cities are Ephesus. Different letters were sent to different cities in order to address different issues particular to that city.

Paul's word choice of assuming or usurping authority over men is very specific. This is to take an office that one was not appointed to. Usurping is a military term, essentially a forceful take over. Paul definitely was not in support of a woman walking into the local church, asserting her dominance, and claiming ownership over the local church body. Women who held high positions in Ephesus before the conversion of the city, are not going to give up their status easily. Nor should a woman (or a man, frankly) just find a group of people without leadership and appoint herself their spiritual leader if unprepared to do so. Particularly so, if the woman did not understand the Scriptures due to her own lack of training or education. Paul's suggestion for the women to become students of the Word was actually countercultural to the time period.

There is a strong difference between a woman who enters into any space only to demand control, authority, and platform in stark contrast to the humble woman who has proven herself worthy and is invited into the space, appointed to her position by others. Paul was ensuring that Timothy understood that not just anyone could lead "the church" in Ephesus. Their societal positions, economic influence, previous leadership, was irrelevant to what was being created in Ephesus. Paul was not going to permit the women of Ephesus to assume authority by proximity to their existing status.

Some, such as author Marg Mowczko believe that Paul's instructions to Timothy were not about restricting all women even in Ephesus, but addressed one woman in particular. Evidenced by the switching of the plural word for "men" and "women" in 1 Timothy 2:8-10 to the singular "man" and "woman" of 1 Timothy 2:11-12. Which holds in context to the latter half of the letter. Paul begins to address very specific issues and concerns happening within the Church of Ephesus instead of a generalized letter to all churches.

Let's also not forget in these very same letters, it is two women to which Paul attributes Timothy's faith. It was the faithfulness and instruction of his mother and grandmother that Paul credited for preparing Timothy for his own appointment. The struggle we face with then with Paul's letters to Timothy is not within the actual Scriptures themselves, but poor interpretation that lacks proper care to context.

CHAPTER SIX:
STRUGGLING WITH
SEMANTICS

In ministry leadership, we have managed to complicate the subject of women in leadership as Christianity branched off to form different denominations. Within these denominations we adopted terminology to define our leadership structures based on our doctrinal beliefs. At times the word choices used by one denomination vary or are even in direct conflict with one another, or the Scripture itself. This lack of a unified accepted vernacular creates obstacles in then determining which roles are available to women and which may not be. For example: There is a church in my state that uses the title of Pastor for men and the title of Minister for women, implying they are different levels of authority. However, in a different denomination those titles are interchangeable for the same position.

We toss around words from denomination to denomination, culture to culture, without care; as well to create loopholes in the system without any regard for how they may add to the confusion and complication. We have also introduced new titles and positions that can not be found within the Bible at all. As the creators of those words, their definition and application fell entirely upon our shoulders, and we decided to whom they would apply. The reality is that the Bible cares more about the character of leaders than setting up complicated leadership structures and hierarchy. The Bible is more concerned with the spiritual condition than the official title. When researching these leadership titles in the Scripture, you will see less of a job description and more attention to qualification.

Semantics in the simplest of definitions is the meaning of words. You may have heard the phrase "it's a matter of semantics", which is used when two people are saying the essentially the same thing (meaning) but using different technical words. An example of semantics is the use of the word Pastor, Minister, Reverend, and Priest. These words by base definition are descriptors of the exact same position in a church, where they vary is between denominations and communities. In some instances you may find that a church uses combinations of these words within their own structures and have applied different meanings which only further complicates.

Complicating circumstances is a very human behavior. Words are tools that we humans use to build and destroy; they include and exclude, we can wield them to manipulate others or encourage. We took it upon ourselves to add to the titles and positions, and then created the rules that would go with them. In doing so, we invited the unintended guest of hypocrisy to the leadership table.

Struggling with Hypocrisy

A very common complaint related to semantics is the hypocrisy of how different titles are used to describe the same position, dependent upon the gender of the person holding the job. In other words, if the position is held by a man the title is Pastor, but if the position is held by a woman the title is Leader or Director. The person holding the position will have the same job responsibilities, same education, and possibly the same pay; it's only their gender that determines the official title. We see this most often in the position of Children's Pastor/Director or Worship Pastor/Leader, where the former is the male leader and the latter the female leader.

Another scenario where this plays out is when a woman wants to apply for a position that is not established in the Scriptures, but is disqualified because someone determined that was a leadership position only available to men. One example of this would be a Youth Pastor position. There is no specified position within the Old or New Testaments or even in early church history that indicates that there was a special pastor calling and appointment for the shepherding of teenagers. Those who created or developed the positions titled it as Pastoral or Clergy, and by default that excluded women from the position.

Of those who have held these alternatively labeled positions, women have shared that there was a direct impact on how they were treated. Pastor, Elder, or Deacon will ensure you are invited to the important meetings or receive respect from the members of the congregation. Whereas Director, Leader, or Coordinator are seen as slightly less than. You may not find yourself invited to the same staff meetings or included in the decision making.

I've heard more than one woman lament over her years spent in a volunteer position, that she was more than qualified for, and when her church decided to hire someone formally into the position, they opted to hire a man and never even offered the job to her. In some instances, the man who was hired had less professional experience, or were external hires and not part of the church membership. There is a level of hypocrisy here (and discrimination) when one suggests that the woman is only good enough to hold the position as an unpaid volunteer. Even more painful for the women holding these volunteer positions that are professionals in that area, serving full time, only to be released so the job can go to a less qualified male applicant. One or even just a few instances of this can be dismissed as poor leadership. The responses from the women in my surveys indicate this is more prevalent and therefore a larger systematic issue.

Hypocrisy plays out on a global scale when a woman is allowed to preach and teach the gospel in the mission field, but not within in home church. If we contend that a woman is not qualified to handle the word of God in our western Christian evangelical church, what value are we putting on the message we send out to the rest of the world? Are we implying that they are only worth second best? What does that suggest about the value of the Gospel to all people? Are we implying that they are not worth the best possible teaching? If she is the right person to send out to other countries, why would she not be equally qualified to share the message in Any Church, USA?

Several of the women from Hearn's contributions were, at least for a period of time, involved in international missions. They experienced the hypocrisy of having a full range of opportunities to serve in the mission field, only to be bound into stricter roles once they were back home. Even when it came to sharing with their supporting local churches the work that was accomplished in the mission field, it would be the male missionaries that would be allowed to address the congregation from the pulpit. Sometimes, it would be delivered by male representatives from the local missionary organization in lieu of the actual female missionary that was actively serving overseas.

Men preach. Women teach. Men deliver a sermon. Women deliver a message. Why are we getting hung up on a word, or title? What difference does it make? This distinction is not only hypocritical, but suggests that women are less than men. Less than is the best way to describe the feeling of being dismissed, disqualified, overlooked, and diminished. It is a feeling that aches within us that, despite all of our gifts, talents, skills, education, training, and calling... that we will always be slightly on the outside... never as good as. Second best.

It is possible that someone reading these words is assuming that I am vying for women to have access to all positions within the church. I want to clarify that my purpose in writing this book was to examine all of the areas where women are being held back from serving in the fullness of their calling. Pastoring is just one of the areas where women are still struggling to serve, but it is probably the area with the most passionate of opinions and part of the conversation that simply can not be avoided. I entered this research with a firm choice to remain objective, only to find that the research is causing my own convictions and traditions to be challenged. This work is as much for myself as for those who will read it.

The goal for this chapter is not to simply challenge convictions and illicit change, but to illuminate the hypocrisy that is found on both sides. I desire that at minimum leaders should be standing firm in their positions. Integrity and credibility stand tall against the hypocrisy of loosely held convictions that are meant to create leeway without yielding any accountability. If your church or denomination believes that women are able to to hold any and all positions within the church, an Egalitarian position, then do your actions match your words? Are you hiring to that standard?

Just the same, if your church holds a Complementarian position that limits women to certain positions, are you standing firm in that conviction? Have you created loopholes to get around doctrinal beliefs without opening up your church to criticism from your denomination or risking disfellowship? If we are going to claim to be of one mind, or the other, we have an obligation to uphold that conviction. It is important to be open and honest about your position. If you should you find your church (or yourself) somewhere in the middle, discovering where you stand or progressing toward one way or another, let this chapter become part of your considerations.

During my surveys, I questioned women whether they felt their church's policies on where and how women could serve were clearly defined. One third responded that their church's policy on women serving was never clearly expressed. You could not find the information online, or among any of the church leadership materials. The only way to know for certain was to ask the church leaders directly. In Kadi Cole's book, *Developing Female Leaders*, she addressed the need for churches to clearly communicate their position on women's leadership to the membership. It's a vague area that our congregations should not have to guess about. As well, when we clearly communicate where we stand from the outset, our potential members can make an informed decision about whether to join our body, which also minimizes confusion and hurt down the road.

Nearing an additional third, the women responded that while their church had a very clearly stated written policy, that was at least partially inclusive of women in some leadership roles, their words did not match their actual practices. A church can claim diversity all they want in word, but if our actions don't match up with our hiring practices and volunteer leadership appointments, then our claims are frankly empty. To not be included is bad enough, to bumble through hypocrisy and never have a solid foundation is much worse. Unsteady, uncertain ground. Never knowing where you stand, or when you might be knocked down.

Last year, I had an opportunity to speak with a woman who was recently promoted for the first time in her church history to a clergy position. She was not give the title of Pastor; in her church that title belonged only to men. Instead, she was given the title of Minister. This was a little surprising, considering that in another denomination the title of Minister is equivalent to that of Pastor. However, within her denomination it wasn't. This was the loophole. No one could accuse their Complementarian church of stepping out of bounds by hiring a woman as a pastor, no one from within their denomination could call for a disfellowshipping. Yet, her job was exactly the same. She was held to the same requirements and expectations.

There are churches that hire women as Women's Pastors, whereas another church would call her Women's Ministry Director. Small Groups Pastors that are women are called Groups Coordinators. Worship Pastors become Worship Leaders. Even if the women have a formal seminary education, their leadership title will be determined by the denomination's doctrine on women. We struggle to know our place in the leadership structure when the structure itself is compartmentalized but also undefined. It's like trying to travel using a map, where the streets have not been named and there is no compass key to show you which way is North.

Back to the Words at Hand

If we want to get to the root of what roles women can serve within the church, we need to have a clear understanding of what positions are Biblical and where women fell in relationship to those roles. The most clear directive was in the Old Testament when the Levitical Priesthood was established, and the priests were male and must come from the line of Levi. Deborah was an example of someone who held an official office of Judge, as well as a Biblical appointment of Prophetess. When we get into the New Testament establishment of the early church, Ephesians 4 lays out the leadership structure in simple terms.

> "And he gave the apostles, the prophets, the evangelists,
> the shepherds and teachers, to equip the saints for the
> work of ministry, for building up the body of Christ, until
> we all attain to the unity of the faith and of the knowledge
> of the Son of God, ... Rather, speaking the truth in love,
> we are to grow up in every way into him who is the head,
> into Christ, from whom the whole body, joined and held
> together by every joint with which it is equipped, when
> each part is working properly, makes the body grow so that
> it builds itself up in love."
> Ephesians 4:11-16

The New Testament established apostles, prophets, evangelists, shepherds, and teachers as the official offices within the church. The **apostles** were a very specific group of Jesus' disciples. To be an apostle you had to meet three criteria, first of which was to be called directly by Jesus. The second criteria was to sit under his direct teaching, and the third criteria required that the person had to be a witness to the resurrected Christ. By this criteria, the original twelve disciples, as well as Paul, were considered apostles. An additional apostle was added to replace Judas, which was Matthias. The apostles did many things such as healing, teaching, sharing the message of Salvation, etc. The core 12 were also the ones who oversaw those appointed into other positions.

Romans 16:7 implies that there may have been other apostles, one of which being a woman. While this is debated, what we do know is that based on the criteria this is an office that is not longer in existence. No one alive today could meet the three criteria to be an apostle. Perhaps, you have seen advertisements for events or church staff listings that include someone with the title of apostle. This is a perfect example of how we have taken terms out of their original context and applied them in a new manner. In this instance, the semantics are that we are using the same word with entirely different meaning.

Prophets and Prophetess were directly tasked with handling the direct word of God, delivering His message to others. In both the Old and New Testaments, women were listed among the Prophets. We are also promised that our sons and daughters will continue to prophecy as the end of days draws near. This was an anointed gift, and not something someone could ascribe to themselves. We read and study the words of Prophets today; they were the messengers of God.

Some would argue in the cases of female Prophets (as well as other positions) was a direct result of there being no *"good, godly men"* available to fill those roles. Talk about limiting the power of the Lord! The Creator of the Universe certainly could raise up a man to lead. God, who can command the dead to rise, could easily have breathed life back into a prophet long dead. God, who creates a new spirit within us, could have easily taken a hardened man and changed him into a godly one. God, who opens and closes wombs, could easily have knit together a male leader to be born for such a time. To imply that God settles for second best by utilizing a woman is frankly a ridiculous argument that laughs in the face of everything the Scripture tells us about Him. Consider this thought from *Recovering from Biblical Manhood and Womanhood,* where Aimee Byrd writes:

"Whenever a strong woman is portrayed in Scripture, teaching or leading a man in any salient way, the popular explanation is often that God is making a point that there were no good men at the time. This argument never holds traction, as well all know God can use Balaam's ass (Numbers 22:21-41) if he chooses. He raise up men, women, and donkeys to carry out his Word." (pg 57)

Our modern day missionaries would be the equivalent of the office of the **evangelist**. It was the commissioning of evangelists to travel to new cities and distant lands sharing the Gospel message to those who had never heard. Paul's letters in the latter half of the New Testament refer to women who were part of his missionary journeys. This role might have been a person's singular calling, or intertwined with other positions such as apostle or prophet.

Shepherds were leaders who were called to tend to the local flock in which they were entrusted. A Shepherd cares for the sheep, making sure they are fed, healthy, and protected. In the spiritual sense, our Shepherds are to make sure that our needs are being met and that we are safe. In some church denominations they have designated different pastoral roles. There is an Executive Pastor who oversees the general welfare of the church, whereas there is Teaching Pastor who is responsible for the spiritual education of the membership. Smaller churches, who may have limited resources or budget, may have a Shepherd-teacher that combines those roles. Larger churches, with more means, may have integrated positions to assist the Shepherd, such as Assistant Pastor, Youth Pastor, Children's Pastor, etc.

There are churches who have held firmly to keeping the Teaching Pastor to men (due to Paul's instruction to Timothy) but allow for women to serve in Executive (or Administrative) Pastoral roles. The Scriptural justification behind this would be the women who helped the spread of the Gospel by financial support, providing their homes, and those who were considered and fulfilled the duties of Deaconesses. Another blended role, the Women's Pastor, is a woman who serves as a shepherd-teacher specifically over the women of the local church.

The **teachers** of the early church bore the responsibility of the faith-based teachings for their church community. Today's Teaching Pastor would vet Bible study materials, research for sermon preparation, and preach during worship services. In large churches, the approval of study materials and overseeing of small groups has begun to fall under a new position of Groups Pastor/Coordinator, who would oversee men and women who serve as individual group leaders or facilitators.

As we progress through the Scriptures, we are introduced to a few additional titles/positions. **Elders** are leaders within the church who participate in preaching and teaching (1 Timothy 5:17). **Deacons** are servants in the church (but would be considered part of leadership) who tend to the personal needs of the members. It is reasonable to expect that as a church grows, so with it grows the needs and responsibilities. A Teaching Pastor will be blessed by an Elder who can carry some of the teaching load, and an Executive Pastor is equally blessed by a Deacon who will tend to the needs of the sick. Depending on your denomination there may be both represented or a blending of the two offices under one title. When it comes to gender, some denominational doctrines open both offices to women, just one, or neither.

Before churches were debating about whether or not women could be a pastor, there were debates on whether or not women could serve as elders and deacons. Romans 16:1 suggests that Phoebe was a Deaconess of the Church at Cenchreae. There are only assumptions about women being considered elders in the Scripture. In fairness, whether male or female, very few who held official offices were named outright. The best evidence that we have that women were filling certain offices in the early church comes from Canon 11 of the Council of Laodicea that expressly forbade women who were considered elders, presbyters, or priests to be officially ordained in the church. This wasn't just a document to answer the question if women could or could not, but instead to close offices being held actively by women at the time.

Over the centuries new positions were added in the church for various reasons. In the early 1940's, the Protestant church employed their first official youth pastor, while the concept of children's ministry dates back at least to the early 1500's. Churches employ administrative assistants, groundskeepers, treasurers or accountants, technical directors, worship leaders, production leaders, and most currently we've added communications leaders that are part of integrated social media teams. Smaller churches may include many of the same positions in volunteer leadership roles, or bivocational pastoral positions. We also have clergy or chaplain positions outside of official churches, including hospital and in the military.

Each denomination, or church, has a description of the position which includes the regular duties and expectations. The overseeing hiring board determines the requirements for eligibility, and the whomever oversees these positions ensures that the job is executed in accordance to the set forth expectations. When it comes to the hiring practices, the most conservative or fundamentalist of churches have established a hard-lined no women need apply position. The more progressive churches will open up a position to anyone who meets the qualifications regardless of gender. In both cases, semantics are not the issue at all. Both define the pastor role as the same, they simply stand in polar disagreement about the inclusion of women. It is cut and dry.

The struggle with semantics and hypocrisy is found everywhere in the middle. When policy isn't clearly expressed, when words are taken out of context and misapplied, or when we have changed the historical definitions of words to better suit our preferences or convictions, then we have muddied the waters and create confusion.

I witnessed two Presbyterian pastors debating over whether or not women could be elders and deacons. A Southern Baptist mega-church recently placed three women into pastoral roles, a move considered in direct violation to the Southern Baptist Convention's doctrine. I sat in a workshop hosted by a SBC church, where a woman led the session. She was introduced as a staff member by the Head Pastor, who informed the audience that as the Head Pastor women could serve in his church in any capacity in which he dictated. In other words, while holding to the position that the Head Pastor must be male, anything else was open game because he was **the guy** in charge. His church, his say so.

If you are a woman applying for employment in a church or ministry, those on the far end of the spectrum are very clear in the job description and requirements what they are looking for. Complementarian churches will exclusively use the words he and him, whereas Egalitarian churches will use she, her, he, him, or they. The churches that fall in the middle of the extremes, or who don't want to publicly state their stance will use vague terms. In accepting applications from anyone who seeks to apply, a committee can then filter out women without anyone being the wiser. It's hard, as a woman, to know if you are wasting your time applying.

Years ago, I applied for a job with a church that was hiring a Women's Ministry Director. With my resume, I included a ministry plan that outlined my overall outlook on ministering to women. I made it through the initial vetting process and to the first interview. The church was located in another state, and so the interview was held over Zoom. I logged in to find a panel of women that were in charge of interviewing me and answering questions I might have about the church or position. After an amazing interview, which felt very promising, one of the women held up a printed copy of my resume and ministry plan. "*I have just one final question, before we conclude...*"

It was at this final moment, that she pointed to the top left corner of the first page of the ministry plan. Right there, in black and white, it stated *"Ministry Plan for Women's Ministry Director/ Women's Pastor"*. This was how I titled the document. She wanted to know why I had included the word pastor. I explained that I had been applying for several jobs that were essentially the same position, some churches considered the position as a Women's Ministry Director, and others categorized it as Women's Pastor. I shared that I was not opposed to applying for jobs under either title. The tone of the interview changed. That word cost me the job. A position of a woman ministering to women, which is Biblical, lost over a word.

Recently, I was having a discussion with a pastor's wife in a neighboring county. It had come up in conversation that a local multi-campus church had couples as co-pastors over the church. The wives were titled Pastor, along with their husbands. My friend shared with me that had not always been the case, but had been adapted in the last couple of years. The reasoning, she stated, was that prior the pastor's wives were not treated with due respect. Once they made the decision to include the wife under the commissioned title of Pastor, the attitude toward the pastor's wives changed dramatically.

Words can make all of the difference. In how women are viewed, treated, and acknowledged.

Semantics matter because words do carry a level of power behind them, not due to the word itself but rather our interpretation and application. We decide which words have value, and we decide which words don't. Words deliver a strong message to others, and can also be used to hide our true intentions. Words manipulate, words can be twisted. Words are used to confirm, deny, and circle around subjects we do not want to address. When we question as to why people get so hung up on words, the answer is in our intrinsic belief that words are important.

As believers, we have implored the world to understand the value of the words that we hold sacred. Which means that we bear an incredible responsibility in handling the Word of God rightly, justly. As ambassadors of Christ, charged with carrying his banner and sharing his message with the World, we must get that message right. Context matters, semantics matter. We cannot lose sight of that in order to protect our opinions, traditions, or doctrine if it is not in alignment with **the** Word.

We struggle with semantics in the area of women in leadership because there is a cost. Someone in this debate is wrong. Someone is going to have to admit that they as an individual, or an entire organization, has made an error. What prevents this kind of truth seeking is pride, arrogance, and fear. Those with the most to lose will only dig their heels in further, unwilling to yield or even move an inch. What would it mean if either of the extreme sides had to admit they were wrong?

For the Complementarians, I believe the most obvious would be a hit to their pride in admitting they were wrong. These deeply held "convictions" would absolutely rock the foundations of their systems. Individual members who fail to agree out of their own patriarchal leanings, would potentially leave the church and take with them their families and tithes. Male leadership would not only fear losing their jobs due to the impact on the church membership numbers, but also fear greater competition in employment if women are included in the applicant pool. Also, for the fundamentalist women in the church, it would result in a shift of responsibility as they can no longer lay their commissioning onto the shoulders of the men. As the woman in Hearn's book stated, it was incredibly convenient to put all the responsibility (and accountability) on the men.

For the Egalitarians, to come to a clear cut answer that is not in their favor would create a wake of unemployment and dismissal of women in leadership roles. They too may face a mass exodus of women (with their families and tithes) as the women struggle to come to terms with the exclusion. Additionally, these congregations that have been dependent on the contributions of women may struggle to bring the men into leadership fold to fill the gaps.

The harvest is plenty, and the workers are few. The real question, I submit, is are we at a point where we can absolve anyone from fulfilling their commissioning? Can any of us afford to bury our talents in the ground? Is it wise for leaders to bind the hands and feet of the body? The days are growing short, the coming of the Lord draws closer. Do we want to be the workers harvesting out in the fields when the trumpet sounds, or unprepared brides asleep in their beds?

As much as they may disagree with one another, it benefits both sides of the debate to let this issue remain unresolved. I'm not suggesting that the influential leaders on each side are conspiring with one another to keep the status quo. Yet, I've not witnessed either side having a willingness to come together and sit at a unified council meeting, like the eras of old, and hash it out in order to find mutual agreement. Instead each side creates the occasional council, committee, or convention to "debate" the beliefs they already hold. Talking in circles, among their own echo chambers.

Those who fall somewhere in the middle find zero tolerance in not taking a side. For the hard lined Egalitarians, those who are progressing toward the inclusivity of women are not moving fast enough. And, for those who are deep in the Complementarian camp, any movement that deviates from their position sets you as public enemy number one. Spend any amount of time on social media platforms, in short order you will witness the arrows slung from either direction.

There are those of us who seek truth. We want to stop struggling over the semantics and instead come together and hash it out. What does the Bible actually say, in context, to the original language? How do we stop arguing the same handful of verses against one another and determine the absolute truth? What does history tell us about the women in the early church, in the very days that pick up where and when the Scriptures stop? What do the immediate years after Jesus' ascension and the original disciples' deaths reveal about the view of women in the early church?

Why Does Any of This Really Matter?

It comes from a genuine desire to be in obedience to the Lord. If the Scriptures support a woman in leadership, then it would be disobedient to ignore our gifting and calling on the basis of our gender. Respectively, if the Scriptures do forbid it with no exception, then it is just as disobedient to step into a role that we are not actually called to fulfill. Those who find themselves caught in the conflict are interested in not obtaining position or title but rather to walk in obedience. It's that simple. A corrupting woman doesn't need resolution; she'll find the weakness and slide her way in. The usurping woman can open up her own church, without a denomination, and teach whatever she deems to be truth.

The faithful woman is asking God to make her calling clear, and to crumble the obstacles that hinder her path. The humble woman seeks not an argument or debate, but clarity over her place. She takes The Great Commission seriously, and seeks to do her part. She is willing to go, as a missionary evangelist. She is willing to baptize, if that is the role given to her. She is willing to teach others, because she has been prepared as she has sat under sound teaching and instruction.

The meanings of prophet, evangelist, shepherd, and teachers are all rooted in one common call... to share the Word with others. The difference is the methodology of doing so, but all were trusted with handling the Word of God in some capacity. It begs to question how a woman could be trusted as a judge or prophet, but not as a teacher or Shepherd; especially considering the teachers of the New Testament were teaching the words of the Prophets. The Bible's vernacular is more than just coincidental, and we are to give it the reverence it deserves.

Shepherds of the day were men, women, and even children. Paul tells Timothy to not allow others to disqualify him over his youth. When the woman with the alabaster jar came to anoint Jesus, he didn't stop her. When the men cleaning out the temple came across a scroll containing the Book of Law, it was Huldah (a woman) they went to for instruction. What is the difference between preaching the Word of God and teaching it? Don't both require the same level of qualification and care? As Hearn's book suggests, we are truly in a deep need of diligent scholarship to resolve the debate, but that must come from neutral parties with objectivity. Those who are willing to set aside their own beliefs, traditions, and doctrines... truth seekers.

I wonder, though, can we ever really resolve this topic when we are still debating about women serving in non-pastoral roles, or about what women can and can not contribute to the church?

In the Catholic Church, men who were called into the dedicated service of the Lord entered the priesthood and women would become nuns. In the Protestant Church, overall there has not been an equivalent space for women. In fact, if you look at the timeline, the further we are removed from the early church it appears that women are finding less and less opportunity. Just last year, I spoke with a female executive team leader within a megachurch on the topic of women's ministry. It was of her opinion that women's ministry was obsolete and no longer needed. She believed that the evolution from in church Sunday Schools into at home Small Groups and Bible studies fulfilled the need that women's ministry once met.

If not there, in women's ministry, then where? If we are closing more doors than we are opening...

Where can she serve in the fullness of what God has created her to be?

I have heard plenty of church leaders proclaim that women have many areas to lead within their churches, but the women responding to my surveys find that to be untrue, more often than not.

CHAPTER SEVEN:
STRUGGLING FOR A SEAT

It was just almost twenty four years prior to this writing, that I made the decision to leave my secular profession and become a stay-at -home mother to our first born. I figured that I would remain out of the workforce for just a handful of years. Because of the expectation that I would return to work at some point, I made to sure to keep abreast of the trends in my industry. This required continuing education regarding the retail industry, leadership trends, and the ever growing and changing topography of internet presence.

Every time that I would begin to consider re-entering the workforce, we were blessed with another child. It became such a running joke, between my husband and I, that we stopped ever talking about my return to work. We didn't want to test God any further. However, this also created an amazing opportunity for me to serve the church. In my early years, while my spiritual skill set was still developing, I had administrative skills that I felt would be valuable to a growing church.

I dove deep into the volunteer pool; you didn't need to ask me twice. Reading and researching, learning and growing. Some seasons, I've found myself on the church grounds every day completing one task or another. Other seasons, I might have been home with the kids during a bit of respite: but all the while I was learning the Word and educating myself about ministry leadership. Once my children were all school-aged, I returned to school for a divinity degree. My goal was to eventually have employment in the church, preferably the one that I was attending.

Despite my dedicated service, growing spiritual maturity, and expanded education... I've yet to achieve this goal. How does one get a job in ministry when the field is already very limiting and the pool of qualified applicants outnumbers the available positions, even more so as a woman? I've been perfectly content serving as a volunteer, even with full time hours. I didn't mind struggling to get a paycheck, so long as I was fulfilled with serving. There are times where my serving was as a member of a team, and not as the leader. I was not bothered in the least. My heart is, and will always be, about the support of the church. Take my talents and put them to use, however I can be of service.

Nonetheless, I still held out hope that one day, there would be a position available for me. A position where my experience, dedication, education, and drive would be a gift to the church to that I had dedicated my life to. When positions within my church became available, I was never ever considered nor even aware they were open in the first place. When I searched outside of my church, I was either the square peg trying to fit into the round hole or one of many applying for the few available spots.

Yet, I sat in a very privileged position. My husband was able to support our family financially; I didn't *need* a job. I didn't have a student loan to repay, as my education expenses were covered by a financial blessing that I can only explain as the handiwork of the Lord. Other women didn't necessarily have this same luxury. They needed a job, insurance, and some desired a ministry job that valued the family in order to provide some flexibility to accommodate their family's needs.

Within ministry, for women, there was limited room for advancement, most relying on either moving from part time to full time or an annual raise to improve their circumstances. When you are working in the church for supplemental income this presents a minimal concern. However, if your income is a necessity it can be difficult to keep up with the cost of living when there are few options available for advancement. The cost of continuing your education can be hard to justify when you are uncertain if it will yield a return on that investment in your future salary (or any salary at all). For many women, they were doing full time work, and not being paid their fair wages. It may be tempting to blame a lack of tithing on low salary rates, but I've witnessed large churches with abundant finances rely on volunteers and unpaid interns instead of hiring staff members into those positions.

When I returned to school for my divinity degree, it quickly became the news of our friend and family circle. Every time I encountered someone, the conversation went the same, as if it were a script that was distributed to all.

Them: "I heard you are going to school for a theology degree!"

Me: "Yes, I am. I'm very excited about it."

Them: "What are you going to do with the degree?"

Me: "I'm not sure yet, but I trust that God has a reason."

This line of questions is normal; most women who got to school for a theology degree are asked that very same question. The answer I gave is also pretty normal. We really don't know what we are going to do with the degree, because we walk in the doors of education knowing that the job market for us is very, very small. The women documented in Hearn's book faced the same concerns. Seeking formal education was not in pursuit of a husband (as some often joke about women in seminary) but for a job, a career, with very narrow opportunities. Men enter seminary with a plan to either enter the pastorate or a career in academia. They don't walk through the halls wondering what they will do when they graduate, whereas women do not have the same confidence over what comes next.

When I pitched this book, I had to provide sample chapters for consideration. A particular acquisitions editor turned down the proposal, telling my literary agent that it just was not the fit for their audience. Imagine my surprise when I received a personal email from that same editor, expressing concern for me. Coming from a denomination that is widely accepting of women in leadership within their church, the editor was concerned about my mental health, how lonely I must feel, and to make sure that I knew there were places I was welcome. I appreciated the concern, but it also added to my grief.

We Do Not Want to Go

For those of us coming from conservative, Complementarian church backgrounds, simply leaving our churches is not a joyful solution. In fact, it's the last thing we want to do. First, we are tied emotionally to our traditions. To leave our denomination means to leave our practices and traditions behind, church won't be the same. We will feel like foreigners in a new church, unaccustomed to their ways. Second, just because we may chose to move on doesn't mean that our entire family will follow. Even if our immediate family transitions with us, extended family may choose to stay behind. They may not want to leave, or even more painfully may not support our reasoning for going. Third, if we have been there for any measure of time we have interwoven into the church family. It's not easy to just walk away from our family and friends. These are people we have grown up with, our children's lives are intermingled, we have build memories with these people. It is a painful severing, and relationships just are not the same after you leave. Last, and what I think was the most important part for me, is that some of us do feel called to facilitate change from within. We want to grow *with* our church family, not *away* from it.

We stay and we pray for change, in the church or in us. If I am wrong about where my research is leading me, I want the Lord to expose that to me and change my heart. If the church is wrong, I want to love her through the unraveling of truth and migrating with change. Walking away is the last resort, but there are those of us who have stayed and prayed long enough. It has become time to go, in order to grow. The suggestion to leave may be the right decision, but that doesn't make it any easier and without its own burdens. Strong women who are leading in the church already struggle to build friendships, and to up and leave under the premise of starting over is not all that appealing. When you are married or have children, you must also weigh the impact of leaving on their relationship and their emotional, mental, and spiritual health.

We are struggling to survive professionally when the church at large is choosing to read Scripture through a 21st century lens, and then applying misconstrued interpretations. Today's women are educated, equipped, and do not suffer under the same types of social or political oppression. We are not called as Christian women to fit into 21st century social patterns but to be reflections of Christlikeness. Christ who was revolutionary in regard to women. We are struggling not just with the Word of God, but our own view of ourselves in relation to God.

People need to feel valued, accepted, and appreciated. Jesus doesn't want us to just survive as women in the church, but to thrive under the authority imparted to us through the royal priesthood of believers. To be overlooked or diminished by our own churches has a psychological impact on our mental health and well-being. Which, we have learned, can manifest in physical impact as well. Women are becoming less concerned about what people think, and more concerned about what God thinks. If God is calling us to lead in a certain capacity or champion a particular ministry, who are we to say no?

STILL HERE AND STILL STRUGGLING TO SERVE

In her book *I Am A Leader*, author Angie Ward writes, *"Finally, after a long season of anguished prayer and reflection, I realized that the problem was not that I was a leader or a woman but that I was trying to deny who God had created me to be. I vividly remember the moment of clarity when I wrote in my journal: I AM A LEADER. From that day on, I committed to the Lord that I would not bury the gifts or calling he had given me.*

I wish I could say it has been smooth sailing since then, but of course, my calling has also been impacted by human systems. There have been times when I have had to hold my tongue, and other times when I have felt compelled to speak up. I have been told by some that my calling is a blessing to the body of Christ and by others that by following it, I am disobeying God. I have felt frustration over the lack of support or opportunity --- and the pain and then freedom of moving to new systems. In the process, God's voice has become clearer, my convictions deeper, and my sense of calling stronger."

As I read through Angie's words, the accounts of the women who contributed to this book, the stories that have been shared with me, and my own experiences ... I see the same words used by today's female leaders as I found scattered in the pages of Virginia's book.

Hurt. Frustration. Lack of support. Lack of opportunity. Holding our tongues. Disobedient. Divisive. Troublemaker. Jezebel. Discontent.

We are still telling the same story of struggle.

With doctrinal lines drawn on the conservative side, Biblical womanhood was defined. Somehow we believed that if we were students of the Word, did our very best, followed the rules, prayed regularly, went to church, didn't rock the boat, and put others first, that it would all end well. We would prove our value and that we were trustworthy. They couldn't deny us the opportunity because we were the model Christian woman. Women who fell into place, following the prescribed stereotypes of female gender roles, still find themselves in marriages that fail. Faithful mothers still contend with prodigal children. The harder women have tried to conform, the more futile it seemed. She doesn't just struggle to thrive, she is struggling to survive.

It's a sobering thought, that today's Christian woman is struggling to survive in her church.

Struggling to Survive

A place that is supposed to bring her to the life-sustaining waters of Christ is pulling her under the waves and crushing her spirit. What does a woman achieve in the present from a life of dedicated service?

During a workshop for women seeking to enter professional ministry or return to the secular marketplace, I asked the presenter:

"How does someone who has been a full time volunteer for the last twenty years, without regular employment structure a resume for returning to work? How does she answer the question about her pay for those volunteer positions? How can we legitimize the volunteer work we have dedicated ourselves to in the church, to reflect our skill sets in the marketplace?"

One of the reasons I was prompted to ask this question came from a woman who was recently widowed and still had children at home. She had elected to leave her career to stay home with her children, as her church encouraged. During these years, she ended up serving in her church as a full-time volunteer. Spread across several different committees, she had been using her skills and gifts to streamline ministry processes across the campus. She bore no title, she was not staff, and this was her gift to the church.

When her husband died, the church to which she gave all of her self had nothing to give back to her. There was no paycheck for the hours of work, no retirement fund, and no contribution to her social security. She had no choice but to seek employment, with virtually no real work history. This made me realize that some times the title is not of personal importance, but professional. Something that can be added to the resume, a title that comes with credibility, a job description that is quantifiable, and can be monetized in the marketplace.

Women are not asking for something they have not earned or don't deserve to be handed over on a silver platter. Instead, they are seeking the validation needed to legitimize the work they are involved in. Even if your church budget can't afford to pay her a wage, you can give her an official position that holds more value to future employers than "*full time volunteer*". Include her in staff meetings, which positions her to tell future employers that she was "*on staff*" and what details that entailed. Setting her up with a seat at the table, in some ways, is an investment in her future even when she's not on the official payroll.

Women who are gifted leaders are asking for a seat at the table, and often find they can't even get invited into the room. Church secretaries and administrative assistants share about being excluded from staff meetings because they are not part of the pastoral team, even when they have information or access to information that would have been helpful during the meetings. One church secretary lamented to me how much time was wasted by not including her within their meetings. She said, "*I know what is coming up the church calendar better than they do. I'm the one with the details about our available budget, what volunteers are out of town, and important deadlines.*" When the pastor would pass on the meeting notes to her after the fact, she commented that the team would end up back a square one after her input. One step forward, two steps back.

When well-equipped, qualified leaders feel left out, they will often step out. High impact leaders won't wait around forever for the invitation to the table. Eventually, they accept the invite to another table or build a table themselves. Evidence for this can be seen in the rise of women's conferences, the Christian women's blog-sphere, self-publishing, social media content, and community-based ministries. Women can join (and lead) within a Bible Study Fellowship or Community Bible Study group; or host events that are open to the public like If:Gathering. These women may not be ready to walk out of their church doors for good, but their volunteer service becomes divided. The more the women feel embraced by these external ministries, the more time and attention they will receive and the church loses.

What is incredibly interesting is that I have observed that once the women have left for another church, ministry, or taken on their own public platform is the reaction of the leadership. If they even notice the woman has left, they sit in shock and dismay. Lamenting to others about how hurt they are that this particular person (and their family) would just leave. They will assert negative opinions over those who leave, judging them harshly as wayward believers who were never "part of us" in the first place. They will criticize the new church over sheep stealing. The leadership will even question or rebuke these women for leading/teaching outside of the authority of the church.

Yet, time and time again, the women I have interviewed have shared exasperation at these criticisms. The signs were there. She attempted to speak with leadership. Her desire was to establish the ministry under the authority and support of her church. She was rejected and dismissed, usually numerous times. In fact, I have yet to meet a woman who started or joined a ministry outside of her church that wanted it that way. She wanted to not only do the work under the authority and with the approval of her pastor, she wanted the ministry to be a positive reflection on her church.

When Christian female bloggers were growing their platforms, this was a result of speaking into an area where women's voices had been mostly silent. Readers welcomed it. Not much has changed as we've added reels and YouTube videos to our repertoire of women-created content about the Bible, ministry, business, parenting, relationships, etc. from the female Christian point of view. Criticized for writing as Christians without any oversight by their churches, concerned about the theology, the target on the backs of women was large and easy to hit. As social media platforms grew, so did the presence of those who desired to stifle women in those spaces. It would be wrong to imply that all women (and men) writing in the public sphere have perfect theology and their interpretation of Scripture is without error. However, I have seen some of the most revered women in theological spaces dressed down as if they were a child at best, and a heretic at worst.

At this table, however, women could speak without interruption. They didn't need to wait for their turn, constantly try to prove their value, they were in control of their space. This was her table. She did not need to be invited, she was seated next to Christ at the head table. She invited other women to join her, other marginalized people. She wasn't withholding, but inclusive. Eventually these women built audiences, attracted publishers, and began large ministries that in some cases spanned the globe. Once women realized they could find obedience in answering God, without worrying about it being within their church walls, everything changed. And yet, criticized every step of the way.

Struggling with Women's Ministry

Another problem that we are facing is that the spaces where we have been historically allowed to serve are being restructured or removed entirely. Over the last ten or so years, there has been a trending concept of "simple church", the idea is to get rid of the erroneous programs and focus on the fundamentals. Women's ministry is often on the chopping block as a ministry that can be expunged. Granted, there are some women's ministries that are superficial coffee clubs and it's understandable to not want to waste budget, manpower, and resources on such a thing. This should not be the fate for the women's ministries that are doing crucial discipleship in the church.

The women won't want to come to church on Sunday, if they are here on Saturday morning.

The women's ministry will become a church within a church, and

STRUGGLING FOR A SEAT

that is out of balance.

Women's ministry is obsolete. Everything that it did is accomplished in other areas of the church now.

If the women attend a weekend long retreat, the men don't come on Sunday with the kids.

Women's ministry isn't even needed here, our women are fine.

The first two concerns have zero data to back up these assertions. A woman who is attending a midweek or Saturday event, is actually more likely to attend on Sunday because of the relationships she is building in her community. I would even go so far as to say that the disconnection of men from their local church bodies is correlated to the dying off of men's ministries, causing the men to lose the communal bonds they once had.

To the notion that women's ministry is obsolete, is also not supported by the data. Women have a far more obligations on their calendar, work hours have shifted from the normal 9-5, and more people are commuting to their places of work. Unless your church is large enough to have a large variety of options for attending studies and activities, those women with more constrained schedules will feel left out. When we create other options beyond the weekly study group, we are providing an opportunity for the women to connect with each other in other capacities. The more women bond with each other, the more secure the community. The more secure the community within the church is, the more dedicated she will be in her attendance and service.

Women are by nature very social, when she can not build relationships within her own church it is not uncommon to build them somewhere else. More than once, I've heard accounts of church leaders not willing to share information with their members about MOPS groups, BSF, CBS, or local women's events held at another church because they fear losing women to the host church. Whether their trepidation is based out of insecurity over their own facilities, worry that a more active church will be more appealing, or even fear that if the women build relationships in those groups they will desire to move to the same church as their new friends; this feeling of threat is very real.

When ever I plan a women's ministry event, it is part of my ministry plan to make room for smaller churches who may not have the funds or resources to host their own events. Special seating is arranged so that the smaller church members can sit together; if breakouts are scheduled, I make sure they are all together. Essentially setting up a Big Sister, Little Sister, relationship between the local churches. I send emails and fliers to the local churches to share with their women's ministry. Rarely is it shared.

Ten years ago, I began a local cohort for women's ministry leaders with the goal of creating a place where we could share ideas and support one another. I created an information brochure with information about the cohort, and included an invite to a meet and greet. We met quarterly for a few years at a local cafe. One morning, a woman saw our welcome sign and inquired about our meeting. I explained the cohort, and she was very interested in attending. She sighed a bit as she said, "*I wish I had known about this sooner!*" Taking down her name and email, I asked what church she attended. I knew the name of this church well; I had personally hand addressed five quarterly invitations that had been mailed to her church. When we had a chance to talk further, I shared that I had sent several invitations already. Visibly annoyed she replied, "*I'm not surprised. My pastor doesn't think this cohort is necessary. He doesn't even think we need a women's ministry.*"

If women's ministry wasn't important, women wouldn't be asking for it. Yet, it is one of the ministries that is put on the sacrificial block for the sake of "simplifying". women's ministry is one area that women can lead fully, without debate, and it's being stripped from her. I don't expect male leadership to understand why women need a ministry that is more tailored to their needs. To disregard it's value simply out of lack of understanding, or to just tolerate it for the sake of keeping women content and quiet, is not correct nor fair. The ease in which it is relinquished speaks to the lack of perceived value.

The message is clear, women's ministry in those churches was never seen as a real ministry anyway.

I can think of a particular church that would invest thousands of dollars, every single year, in Vacation Bible School. The kids who would end up being baptized were always existing members of the church. The children who attended from the community at large would not be seen again until the next summer. Yet, the church would continue to invest in this ministry because they saw it as valuable seed planting, even if they were never going to see the harvest. In this same church, their women's ministry was growing, bringing in new members (and families) to the church. Women's study groups were increasing in attendance size and more becoming available. The women's ministry did not take a single dime from the church, it was completely self-sustaining. When the church decided to slim down their programs, thanks to the simple church concept, the women's ministry was the first thing to go.

Women's ministry is not the only area where we are experiencing a pull back. In my own community, I have watched as food pantries have shut down, and the community has been referred to the state run food program. A church that partnered with two local schools in providing Thanksgiving meals to families in need stopped contributing directly. It was easier to just write a check. With their disassociation they not only handed off the blessing of giving, but also the blessing of serving. The woman who led that program for decades was devastated. A local "Family Closet" which provided clothing for those in need, as well as to foster parents, was disbanded. Another church ended their school supply drive. All of these were programs that were coordinated by women and their volunteer force was primarily female.

Struggling in Academia

In 2018, a man wrote to the Desiring God website, asking John Piper if it was prudent for women to be professors at seminary. The nutshell answer that Piper delivered was a resounding no. Piper suggested that in a seminary the position of the professor is essentially equivalent to the pastoral office, and therefore inconsistent with the scriptures to allow her to hold such a position.

He proposed that if a woman teaches a man in preparation for his pastoral role, then that man is influenced by her thinking and interpretation. His teachings would be tainted with her influence, thus those who sat under his teaching would by proxy receive her teaching. Let's consider the fact that the Scripture that Piper uses to disqualify women from teaching, in Paul's first letter to Timothy is followed by a second letter where Paul credits the teaching of Timothy's mother and grandmother for his theological development and faith.

She can't lead a women's ministry because it's either obsolete or a threat to the church. She can not teach at a seminary because her teachings would infiltrate the body through the pastor. She can not hold the office of Pastor. What is left for her? The answer from many who stand in opposition to women in leadership roles would suggest that there are still many opportunities for serving. Hospitality, children's church, the nursery. Domesticity. The same opportunities women have always had. The needle hasn't moved.

What if hospitality is not her gifting? What if she's not of the right temperament for children's ministry? What if she is a woman who desires children but cannot conceive, and serving in the nursery is a painful experience for her? It is not wrong for a woman to want to serve in these spaces, and to make them available to her. I am thankful for the women who are gifted and anointed to work with children, who have a talent for making food that speaks love into the souls of others, and those who minister in practical ways.

However, I do not support relegating all women to these positions or assuming by gender alone they are qualified for these positions. In as much, I would also defend this argument for the men who are gifted with domestic talents. Men who have run soup kitchens and recovery ministries, men who find joy in serving on

Sunday mornings in Children's Church and take a week off from work to volunteer for VBS or camp. Trust me, if you had to choose between my husband as a Kids Camp volunteer... he is the man for the job.

When it comes to leaders, the book *Church Refugees* points out that the statistics show the greatest exodus from the church is long-term leaders who feel overlooked and dismissed. If you want to send a clear message to someone about how you value their contribution, complete dismissal is one of the most obvious. I've listened to the heartbreak of women who can not get their pastor to even meet with them to discuss ministry leadership, as well as the ones who stepped up to help or lead and were completely dismissed.

Women will offer up their skill, knowledge, and experience to help benefit the church, only to have it turned down. When dismissed, they rarely will challenge it. Those who do challenge are often labeled a Jezebel or a troublemaker. Women are conditioned to not rock the boat, to be a peacemaker, and keep their head down and be quiet. I recall being called "divisive" because I didn't agree with a ministry decision, without even being able to defend my perspective. Women who feel cast aside, won't speak out. The fear is too great. Women do not want to risk losing the gains they have made; she fears being blacklisted. Threat of repercussions silence the women.

We should be very concerned that women experience fear of speaking out in their churches.

If women are not being invited to the table...

If women are being kicked out of the table where they once sat...

If women are being excluded from the room, the conversation...

How then do they lead like God created them to?

If Not Here, Then Where?

The realization that not everything had to fall under the authority of the church or their pastor, changed everything. Ministries were being built and run in communal spaces versus within the church halls. Women were becoming comfortable with starting up their own ministries, creating websites, and building teams to serve alongside. The rejected were feeling fulfillment and found community with each other.

This has been to the detriment of the church. Instead of having educated women (professionally and theologically) serving in the local church, these women are serving elsewhere. When you consider that the majority of the volunteers used by the church to operate consists of women (in some cases up to 85% or higher), what happens to the church when she takes her gifts elsewhere? What message do we send to their children, when the establishment of the church implies that their mother is less than or has less to contribute? Especially to their daughters?

Why would future generations of women want to lead, or even attend, a church where they feel less than? When the statistics show that the current generation of young adults (and those emerging into adulthood) are desiring to be connected into communities where they are doing meaningful work, and making an impact... if it's not available in the church... then in what community will they land and call home?

With women making up the largest percentage of attendees on any given Sunday, what message do we send to the single women, divorced women, retired women, and widowed women about their place and contribution to the church? What message are we sending to the women who are graduating seminaries with theological degrees? How do we serve the women who have experienced trauma at the hands of men, in a church where only men are in authoritative positions?

Women do not want to survive in church, they want to thrive and contribute to the expansion of the Kingdom. Volunteers will serve with longevity and commitment, when serving within their gifting and passion. When allowed to serve or lead within those ministries, they do not mind stepping out and helping in the other areas without threat of burnout. They are refueled in their passion areas to serve in the places where we simply need holes filled.

Women really don't want to build their own tables, but to be invited to a seat at the table that already exists. They want to serve under the authority of their church, and as a representative of their church. A deep desire exists in our very souls to do something that is impactful for the Kingdom. We do not want to sit by and do nothing, knowing that we have something of value to commit. When continually dismissed or set aside, eventually you will reach one of three outcomes.

The first outcome is complete **disassociation**. She gives up completely, defeated. Her volunteering will come to an end, she will show up and go through the motions because she is invested in the community of her church. Not leaving entirely, her attendance becomes spotty as she's more apt to miss a service. The second outcome is that she will **disband**, taking her gifts and talents somewhere that will value the contribution. This might be a new church, para-church ministry, or within the community. She will grow and find fulfillment there.

What is not talked about enough is the emotional and spiritual toll that this type of dismissiveness takes on her. She will struggle with God over why he would make her this way, give her these skills just to be discarded. She will toil with the disappointment in the men (and sometimes other women) of God whom she trusted, and the amount of hurt and trauma she will carry will drag her down. Future relationships within the church will come with skepticism, cynicism, and a deep lack of trust.

When this happens enough, the third outcome is **deconstruction**. She will begin to deconstruct the faith systems that she was raised in. In some cases this becomes a deep dive into apologetics, history, theology vs. doctrine, and a true desire to know the absolute truth of God's promises to her. Not all deconstruction ends this way; for some the pain is so enormous that their entire faith system is rocked and distrust for the institution of the church is beyond repair. We are watching deconstruction unfold in the public sphere, present day. In addition to the term deconstruction, we have also met with the ex-evangelical who still loves God but not the systems of the stereotypical evangelical church.

Perhaps, we are in a season of refining fire, where only the best of the church will be what remains. Something that looks different from what we have become accustomed to in the last few decades and bears a strong resemblance to the early church, where the mission was sharing the Gospel and not protecting traditions.

Perhaps, we are tearing apart the old tables and rebuilding something better. Tearing apart is messy work, even when the final product is stunningly beautiful.

CHAPTER EIGHT:
STRUGGLING WITH HOPE

Women are still clinging to the hope that things will not always be this way. It is a struggle to hold on so tightly, but sometimes that is all we have... hope. Hope that opportunities will arise and doors will open. We hope that the stained glass ceiling will shatter, the glass cliff will be a thing of the past. We hope that our gifts and talents can be received as a blessing. Whether it be a volunteer leadership position, or as a full time paid staff member, she holds to the hope that one day she can contribute to her family's income while equally serving in the passion God has set ablaze in her heart. She, too, is thinking of the legacy she will leave for her granddaughters. Are we still *"emerging persons"*, just as Hearn felt? At what point do we get to celebrate that we have emerged. Finally.

Author, Douglas S. Bursch shared on Twitter this encouragement: "God values his voice in you. Others should as well. Healthy Christian environments will value the voice of Christ in you. My dear sister in Christ, it is your eternal birthright to proclaim the good news of Jesus. Keep speaking. Those with ears to hear will listen." We need more men speaking up for us, speaking up for those who can't. Lending their voice to our cause is an enormous validation.

Reverend Lauren Harris shared with me an experience that was highly troubling. In her early years of ministry development a male friend invited her to dinner with one of his mentors. She shared the the conversation took a unexpected turn, and frankly what was said was so grossly inappropriate I struggled with whether I should... and even could... include the exact verbiage within this text. I was not surprised by it, mind you. Even with a bit of editing to tone down the verbiage, I just wasn't certain that the limited space in this text would allow for the full nuance of her experience to be explored.

Yet, something kept gnawing at me. After a few days of sitting with her story, letting it stew in my thoughts, I followed up with her. I was interested in what her male friend, who was also in ministry, did in the moment of this exchange. She was the victim of sexism, misogyny, and just down right vulgar disrespect as not only a woman but a child of God, imago dei. Did her friend speak up, defend her, correct his mentor, or sit by and allow this to happen unchallenged and unrebuked?

Rev. Harris said that he did apologize after the fact, but during the conversation he just sat there. She was angry and even stated that she was blindsided by the kind of man her friend considered a mentor. The friend was in his early 20s and an associate pastor at the man's church. She didn't think that he wanted to challenge him. I tried to imagine myself in his shoes. What would I do? What would I say?

His response revealed that the men who support women in leadership positions, whom we might call an ally, are equally afraid to stand up and challenge their predecessors. They too fear reprimand, blacklisting, and do not want to upset or offend those who they consider their mentors. Progressive men will quietly make pathways open, encourage their sisters, but to publicly rebuke could come with a cost they are not ready to pay.

With websites dedicated to exposing *false teachers,* and the reality of our current cancel culture, these fears are not unfounded.

When Saddleback Church ordained three women into ministry, the news traveled quickly, and in short order there were calls for disfellowshipping from with the denomination. Easily this could impact not only the careers of those leaders who have established larger platforms, but alignment or agreement could impact those leaders who are just emerging. All journeys have a cost. The woman's journey into leadership has no promise of ease or comfortability, the men defending that journey have no promise to not be caught in the crossfire.

Whenever those in my immediate circle of friends and mentors are about to step into a new season of ministry, one of us will usually speak up asking if she has "considered the cost". This is a reminder that no movement for the Kingdom goes unnoticed. The enemy sits like a lion outside our doors ready to devour. The more we work, the more he tries to undermine. He will unleash all of his forces upon us to deter us, no one that we love is spared. The Word promises us that no weapon formed against us will prosper, but we are not promised that we will end the battle unscathed.

It can be a struggle to hold to hope when it seems like the odds are stacked against you. Kadi Cole, author of *Developing Female Leaders,* has been invited to cross the thresholds of churches nationwide to illuminate to leaders to the value of the women in their midst. In her Facebook Group, Ministry Chick, there is a regular featured post called "Good Guy Spotting" where the women in the group share the moments when they have found themselves, or witnessed other women, receiving support and encouragement from their male counterparts. This happens mostly at a smaller more intimate scale, but there are those who feel secure enough to take the risk. We are thankful for these "good guys".

While not all of our allies are public figures who have amassed platforms, there are amazing men that are going above and beyond to create space for the women in their churches to thrive in leadership. I do not want this book to leave you feeling hopeless. I refuse to compile a catalog of depressing stories without reminding that even though the needle hasn't moved much as a whole, that does not mean there isn't more significant movement in the smaller niches of women's experiences.

The youngest women's ministry leader that I have ever met was just 18 years old. I was invited to speak at one of her women's brunches. At the conclusion, I had the opportunity to speak with their pastor before I left to return home. I mentioned how impressed I was with her as their women's ministry leader, and he said *"We recognized her anointing at a very early age, probably 8 or 9, and we've been preparing her ever since."*

There is something to be said about leaders who are not just recognizing the anointing of women, but intentionally investing into the development of leadership skills as women in the church. Even more so encouraging to see this happening at such young ages. I think to the woman who reminded me that we are paving a way for the next generation, and I do not want to do those women a disservice while staying the course that women of today are not capable leaders either.

I recall being once told that I was in Ministry Middle age, too old to be seen as relevant and too young to be seen as sage. The idea that a woman in her 40's is in a no man's land of leadership seemed absurd to me. I tested out the information on a few other leaders I encountered. At first, they would buck against the idea. Yet, as they fleshed it out, they realized there was at least an element of truth. Where do I find the majority of women in their 40's serving? Outside the church. All women need liberating, freedom to serve as they are created, and age shouldn't be a factor.

Let us not lose sight, as well, that men need liberating too. Just as women have been forced into a mold or stereotype of "biblical womanhood", so have men been forced to fit into the tropes of "biblical manhood". I have been very fortunate to be married to a man who is the absolutely complement to how God crafted me. His strengths are exactly what my weaknesses are, and my strengths only help to lift him up. He is not intimidated or hindered by my strengths, but welcoming of them. He is my champion. I can do all that God commissioned me to because of my husband's willingness to support that calling.

One evening, I was overwhelmed by this journey. Tears were streaming down my face because of how hard it was. What I wanted was something easy, not to be blazing trails and challenging the patriarchy. I wasn't interested in fighting for more, I just desired what was right and fair. *"Lord, lead me to a church who needs a women's ministry Leader. I don't care if I get hired, just let me serve your daughters. I don't need anything more than that."* I cried out. It was my husband that pushed, pressed, and encouraged. He told me to mop up the tears and recognized that the Lord called me to more than that. In fact, these battles are the very things that God has created me for. Giving me the eyes to see, ears to hear, and mind to be aware of the iniquities that still exist; but also the voice to speak to it. He said, *"If it was easy, anyone could do it. But it's not, and that is why God gave it to you."*

Women, like us, are able to keep pressing forward because of the men in our lives who see what others are missing. These fathers, husbands, brothers, and pastors who are not beholden to ego or what someone else defines as masculinity; they hold open doors and stand to our defense. He is honored to be home with the kids, while she walks in her purpose. He opens his platform to her, while she speaks from her strength and expertise. He packs favor bags and hangs floral arrangements at her event, because he wants her to succeed and sees the value of her calling. He is not afraid to be the stay home dad or manager of the home, if it means that she stands in obedience. He arises and calls her blessed, and he is given honor at the city gates because of all she is.

We are able to conquer our racecourse through the encouragement of the women who surround us and support each step we make forward. Just like a marathon runner has a person handing out water to the runner passing by the check point, we have friends and mentors who dish out to us wisdom as we run the race set before us. The friend who picks us up, wipes off our knees, bandages them, and sets us back on course. The friend who stands on the sidelines holding a homemade poster reminding us that we were made for such a time as this. The friend who believed in us so much, she paid the entry fee when our budget was sparse. The coach who runs along side us encouraging us to take one more step. The cheerleader who stands across the finish line, locking eyes with us to help us focus as the race draws to a close.

In *Our Struggle to Serve*, many of the women pointed out the dichotomy between how women responded to Paul versus Jesus. Women often feel battered by Paul's words, whereas in Jesus they feel accepted. Paul restricted women, Jesus defended women. It is a surface level, even visceral response, that fails to see the nuances of Paul's words and understand their place in the Biblical narrative. In Beth Allison Barr's book, *The Making of Biblical Womanhood*, Chapter Two begins with a three-word exclamation: *"I hate Paul!"* Barr explains that this was a common sentiment from mostly female students, who she described as scarred from the way Paul's words were wielded against them as a weapon of control. When used incorrectly, Paul's words can feel anything but hopeful and stand in stark contrast to Jesus' inclusionary language and behavior toward women.

To really understand what Paul was trying to convey, we must learn to distinguish between the local, cultural, elements of the time and deeper theological principles.

If we take into account:

- the timing of the Scriptures, where women were less educated and less equipped

- the culture itself at the time, where it would have been offensive for women to lead

- the patterns of marriage at the time, which were suppressive to women at the time

Barr later in her chapter poses the following: *"So here is my question to for Complementarian evangelicals: What if you are wrong? What if evangelicals have been understanding Paul through the lens of modern culture instead of the way Paul intended to be understood? The evangelical church fears that recognizing women's leadership will mean bowing to cultural peer pressure. But, what if the church is bowing to cultural peer pressure by denying women's leadership? What if, instead of a "plain and natural" reading, our interpretation of Paul – and subsequent exclusion of women from leadership roles – results from succumbing to the attitudes and patterns of thinking around us? Christians in the past may have used Paul to exclude women from leadership, but this does not mean that the subjugation of women is biblical. It just means that Christians today are repeating the same mistake of Christians in the past – modeling our treatment of women after the world around us instead of the world Jesus shows us is possible."* (page 41)

We see that our hope gets lost when we attempt to apply narrowed twenty-first century application to historical texts. The truth is that Christianity was revolutionary for the times. Women were hosting the church in their homes (Colossians 4:15), holding prayer meetings and prophesying (1 Corinthians 11), serving in various capacities (Philippians 4); from deacons (Romans 16) to financial patrons (Luke 8:3).

One of the charges from *Our Struggle to Serve (page 173)*, is that it is our task to not fit our twenty-first century selves into first century social patterns. Instead, we need to live in the twenty-first century, and closely scrutinize where we should stand against society, where we should follow the normal behavior patterns, and where we can modify our stance based on our conscience. With the right view, we can act on our callings without fear.

We must hold on to the hope of things to come, the good guys, and the opportunities that are becoming available in order to prevent ourselves from becoming jaded. The needle has not moved much as a whole, but it has moved in some areas quite significantly. Women are finding places in vocational ministry and seminary teaching roles, just not at the pace to meet the supply of educated women available. Let's not lose sight of the wins that we resign ourselves to wallow in the losses.

Women want to be be released to serve in the capacity in which they were created. She wants to be seen as whole and capable of making decisions and leading others well. We demean her when we ask her if she has the permission of her husband or family to step into leadership or volunteer in a particular way. This was a point noted several times within the original text in *Our Struggle to Serve*, indicating this is an area that has not changed much in the last fifty years. When do women reach the point where they are fully capable of making important decisions without having to run that by the men (father, husband) in their lives? And, frankly, why do those in leadership assume she wouldn't have already consulted or at least planned to? In a good marriage, it is rare that either the husband or wife will make a big decision without discussion.

Women are struggling to see the hope of a future in ministry leadership, when we are still stumbling through the same tropes that have been shilled out for decades. She doesn't seek to become a Jezebel, but rather walk in obedience. She doesn't dare to go against His Word, but rather find her place within it. She agonizes to accept herself as she is, in a predominantly male society. Which is a wild concept to accept when we understand that statistically this is not so, with men globally edging out women as a majority by less than half a percent. Within the church, women are the dominant gender. Which returns my thoughts to my husband's question of why we allow ourselves to be treated this way.

Hope is not lost, however, its just fighting for its' place. We are having these conversations because people need to be aware. I, personally, spent too much time thinking that I was the only one facing these issues and taking it personally. When I realized this was an issue that extended beyond me and wasn't just debating over the pulpit, but really a larger scope of women in general leadership positions within the church, it made all the difference. A person is not troubled by what they are unaware of, but once they are made aware of it, they can no longer avoid it. The waters become troubled.

Cultural conditioning, including sex stereotypes and perceived gender norms, steer us all toward known and familiar, without challenging the accuracy of those directions. Church and cultural conditioning suggested that marriage and kids were the goal for women, her husband was part of her identity and she found her status in him. These pressures stole hope and instead smothered her in worry and anxiety. Am I sinning if I am using my God-given gifts in a way that is counter to what society or church leaders have taught? Or, am I sinning if I am content falling in line with these traditions while ignoring my gifts and being disobedient to God? The tension between these questions is a millstone around our neck.

At the time of Hearn's book, it was recognized that the conservative church and the media were deliberately attempting to keep women preoccupied with housekeeping and being attractive for men.

Strong, independent women were unconventional. In our current culture, when evaluating our current marketing campaigns, it is evident that much has not changed. The beauty, self-care, and household industry is the fifth highest globally; beat out by food, tobacco, pharmaceuticals, and crude oil. Our emerging generation is challenging these conditions, but we still have more growth to come.

There is this belief that if you work hard, do your best, follow the rules, you are going to live happily ever after. If marriage and motherhood is the greatest calling, and women are setting aside their own ambitions or purpose in order to be the best wife and mother... why are marriages still failing? Why are kids wayward? It does not make sense.

When she entered the marketplace, she was told a lie that being a wife or mother was not compatible with success. So, she chooses domesticity and loses herself in the process, and her marriage ends. She chooses career only to find herself as the blame when there is a corporate disaster (even if she was hired to mitigate that crisis as part of the glass cliff). When she was uneducated, she wasn't smart or skilled enough. Now she is too smart and too successful for her own good. Dr. Marion Hillard suggests that if a woman disregards her personhood, then she will become whatever the culture demands for her to be.

The church's opinion on her significance or how she contributes matters to her. So, if Hillard is correct, she then disregards her personhood and conforms to the church's demand for her. The attitudes she encounters will have profound impact on how she will see herself not just *in* the church, but also *out* in the world. If she doesn't feel like she is a valued contributor to the church, if she feels like she has not be shepherded well, or that she is lacking in some capacity, then her confidence to impact the world in which she has been placed will be compromised.

She struggles with hope, because she struggles with being misunderstood. She does not want to take from, but contribute to. The overwhelming assessment of the reaction of men to women in ministry leadership comes down to the root of fear versus and openness to change. Even if we can not come to an agreement about the top tier pastor roles, we should be able to come to an agreement on all of the other areas where women are rejected.

I once posted on Twitter an account of a woman's struggle leading Bible Studies in her church. Despite the fact that several women expressed similar struggles, many of the men who responded copped an attitude of *"that doesn't happen in my church, so it must not really be an issue"*. It is similar attitude that we saw on display in the #MeToo, #ChurchToo movements; as well as in relation to general sexism and racism in social, marketplace, and church spheres. It is wrong to be dismissive of someone's experiences, especially when they are supported by others, just because *you* are not that kind of pastor or leader.

To love they neighbor as we love ourselves does not mean we can just deny our sister's experiences because they make us uncomfortable. Shared experiences are not required in order to sympathize, empathize, or recognize that there is indeed a problem to be addressed. It would be altruistic to think that we could just read a book, or ten, sit down and have a few conversations, and wake up the next day to a cohesive view on women in leadership. This is a conversation that will take time with a genuine desire to seek the right answer without bias of our own beliefs and traditions.

A hard truth is that society, and even the church, will never value women in the same way that God does. Life in Christ means freedom for men and women alike, in a world that wants to bind us to constraints and constructs. We are captives set free, in order to be all that we can be within our relationships to others and in service of our King. It is time to retire the idea that our greatest calling is being a wife or mother, and instead accept that perhaps our greatest calling varies based on what our gifts, talent, and purpose are.

In *Our Struggle to Serve,* we find a hope that we can still hold onto even amongst our struggles today. "God's love for me didn't depend on whether I could work for him or not – and it didn't depend on the acceptance of other Christians." (*Our Struggle to Serve, pg 70).*

You may never find a full-time job or lifelong career in
ministry, but God loves you anyway.
You may never find the acceptance of your gifts by others,
but God loves you anyway.
Don't lose sight on this. Ever.
God loves you.
As you are.
Right now, in this moment.
Not because of what you do.
Because of who he is.

We must hold on to the hope found in the promises of the Lord. When man or tradition may want to confine women, Jesus sets them free. When men try to send her out of the room, Jesus welcomes her to serve him as she washes his feet with her tears and dries them with her hair. When men attempt to accuse her, Jesus asks those without sin to cast the first stone. When the men attempted to send her away, she persisted and Jesus commended her faith. When she dared the boldness to touch the hem of his garment and Jesus then healed her. We cling to these words, hope-filled words that in Him, all things are possible for those trust.

When we give our lives to God, He returns to us our true selves. Refined and redeemed. We are not an empty shell. We are individuals with our own gifts, talents, and purposes. We are sanctified through Him. While we may long for the encouragement and acceptance of our church, we only need to have confidence in His love and acceptance of us. We may be struggling, but that doesn't me we stop hoping.

CHAPTER NINE:
DON'T TAKE MY WORD FOR IT

It would be irresponsible of me to build an entire book on the topic of struggling to serve in the modern evangelical church based on my own experiences or stories that I tell second-hand. In the coming pages you will enter the worlds of other women who have or continue to struggle to serve. I am beyond humbled to be trusted with their words.

In compiling these stories, it was important for me to find perspectives that represented different denominations, cultures, traditions, and views. Their inclusion is not meant to endorse or repudiate a specific denomination or belief system. Instead, the intention is to show that the struggles faced are not limited to a particular myopic group but widespread across the landscape of Christianity.

Out of respect for the risk that comes with speaking openly, contributors were given the option to reveal their full name, identified by their initials, or complete anonymity. I pray that you read these words with an open heart, and open mind. If a particular story triggers an emotional response, ask the Lord to reveal to you how to process that emotion and what you can do next.

However, if a story triggers a traumatic response, please pass those pages by. This book is intended to help, not to rub salt in wounds or revisit painful history. To bring us toward understanding and move toward healing, we can't not avoid the hard parts. However, you can choose to be kind to your own heart and save these pages for another day.

AUDRA SHANEMAN
A Woman's Struggle

"Unfortunately, after about thirty years of volunteer service in Christian churches, the roadblocks of doubt and suspicion have damaged my enthusiasm for ministry and decreased my ability to fully support the current church model of ministry.

According to Who Volunteers in America, women are more likely to volunteer than men, and in churches this is also true. Funeral service groups, Sunday School teachers, and Awana leaders are in the most cases women. Yet, in the last three churches I attended there has been no intentional ministry target to help this demographic. Yes, men's groups are necessary and no doubt the condition of masculinity, fatherhood, and getting men to church is of utmost importance. I believe the Spirit of God can empower and inspire more than one ministry. In all of these churches, women served, but were not considered valuable enough to serve. Ouch.

I fully support MOPS, women's bible study groups, women's retreats, volunteer recognition and appreciation, meal trains, and all the valuable activities that contribute to serving women and supporting their relationship with God. The lack that I see is support for women's purpose and opportunity to impact her world. Yes, if she is married and with children there is priority there and managing her home. However, according to one study, 50% of women are the breadwinners in their family. This is a major shift in our families, homes, and society. Yet, the church is woefully unprepared to address and minister to this shift in roles for both men and women.

Regardless of how this shift came about or whether your pastor agrees or not, this is the mission field. Churches used to depend on stay at home moms to organize, carry, and implement much. Women who had sense of purpose, a desire to grow, and a mind to make an impact would fulfill these roles. But, when educational and vocational arenas opened up, it wasn't Pandora's Box. It was opportunity.

In my early twenties, I was single and exhibited leadership and organizational skills. I ran a sports ministry for a very large church with at least 500 participants. Was this activity vital in growing my relationship with God? No. It was a job that needed to be filled by a stable and responsible person.

By my early thirties, I was single in a church without women's gatherings for support, encouragement, and community. With a small team, we started to do regular brunches with a meal and some encouragement. However, the pastor also connected me with older women who were instrumental in my development as a Christian and a woman. He was open to who I was, not attempting to squeeze me into something he was comfortable with. This is key for women who struggle to serve. There is no lack of needs, there is lack of understanding that women are not resources to use but people to grow and flourish.

I moved and came under the headship of another woman in a new church plant. There were some opportunities to serve, but the feeling I got was that only certain gifting and expressions were needed. If you were not a great musician or a great speaker, you had to seek opportunities elsewhere. Sadly the church had a split that was not easy, pretty, or without collateral damage.

Our next church, as a family, was in a church where ministry to women flourished. The pastor's wife was an active partner in the ministry and respected as a skilled teacher of the Bible. This example of "success" as a woman serving alongside her husband was not lost on me. It was really his choice, but also great wisdom to receive and release his wife into these opportunities.

We moved again, and our latest church experience was one of the most damaging in my struggle to serve. This was a new church plant, and we felt called as a family to be a part of it. I was asked to give the announcements and lead prayer on rotation. I felt that this was a moment where I was acting in my calling, a place where God had gifted me. Unfortunately the Head Pastor, would not encourage or even look at me when I was finished. There was no acknowledgment from the pastor of the anointing, or contribution I made to the service. Whether it was personal insecurity or a lack of experience, this felt like a brick wall to me.

I have a Bachelor of Science degree in Biblical Studies. Not that education is required for effectiveness, but I had more theological education than 95% of the men in the church. To one leader, this would be seen as an asset. To another leader, it's viewed as a liability.

But through this experience, I realized the deep need for approval versus affirmation. I had been looking to the pastor for approval, when I had that from God. The affirmation, the blessing, receiving my gifts, etc. was given and this is the lesson of why I am writing about my struggle to serve.

When leaders receive the gift coming to them, understand it, and then release the gifts to grow, I believe the church will experience greater vitality and impact. When a leader sees the responsibility as a shepherd to not only speak at the people from the pulpit, but to know the sheep and assist the sheep in what they are called to do, impact also grows.

Leaders without vision and understanding about their own purpose will struggle to receive and release. My gift is not condemnation of yours. My purpose is not a denial of yours. Our churches struggle because of a lack mentality instead of an abundance mentality. Honestly, there is enough need in this world for highly functioning Christians that to not receive and release those with ovaries is so short sighted.

I expect the church to treat women differently than the world. If I see the same stifling of women in a body, I expect that they are also stifling the Holy Spirit (which dwells within her). How do we receive those who have been brought near by the blood of Christ? Are they resources to be used up or are they gifts to open, discover, and release into the world?

It is my hope that the church doesn't just relegate you to bringing a cake.

My daughter has seen her mother's skills be dismissed and unfortunately my hurt and frustration. I will encourage her to seek Christian friends, groups to study the Bible with, and a place where she serve. But honestly, I fear that she will take her God given gifts and talents and offer them to the world instead of the Body of Christ. Just as I would tell her to not marry a man who does not appreciate who she is, I would tell her to not sit in a pew where she is not received as a new creation and released.

Tradition tramples along and women will be seduced with the "doing for God" to earn man's approval instead of serving confidently out of His approval.

As in the story of the woman who pours oil on Jesus' feet, weeps on them, and then wipes them with her hair; many women are so grateful to Jesus for His acceptance and affirmation. We know that we have been saved, and we believe Ephesians 4:11-16, which says:

And he gave some apostles, and some prophets, and some evangelists, and some pastors and teachers; for the perfecting of the saints, for the work of the ministry, and the edifying of the Body of Christ. Till we all come in the unity of the faith and knowledge of the Son of God, unto a perfect man, unto the measure of the fullness of Christ.

Many women believe that the fullness of Christ has not yet been achieved. Many women are prepared and anointed to work towards this end by the Power of the Holy Spirit."

ANONYMOUS

Struggling with a Broken Heart

"For nearly thirty years, I have said yes. When asked to lead a ministry, I said yes. Run to the store and pick up some items for the Sunday morning Sermon illustration, I said yes. Would I mind filling in for the secretary while she is on vacation, I said yes. I've said yes to so many things, so many requests. Come in early to set up? Yes. Could I stay late and help clean up? Yes.

I've served within my passion and my calling, and I've manned up to serve in the ones that are not. Stints of leading Vacation Bible School in the craft room, checking in new families when they arrive on their first Sunday morning, these are not part of my spiritual gifts. But, much like the mantra of the movie Robots, if I see a need then I fill the need. It was my pleasure and honor to step in and help serve the church in whatever capacity they needed, in whatever way I could. Upon arrival home from whatever activity I was wrangled into, I would tell my husband in exasperation that I was never going to do that again. Only to answer the call the next day, the next week, the next month, and the next year. Year, after year.

When I was able to serve in my passion, I was on fire. There was no stopping me. Whether it was in women's ministry, MOPS, Drama Ministry, leading Bible Studies, or contributing to leadership training. That is when I would light up. The world felt good and right when I was standing in my calling and purpose. It was in doing this that I was filled and fueled up, making it easier to say to all of the out of my wheelhouse requests. I could serve outside my calling to the point of exhaustion, drained to my core, because I would instantly feel full again when I was serving how the Lord called and crafted me to be.

Yes, I will pick up that weird item from some obscure store across town. It's not a big deal, since the following weekend I'm serving the Daughters of the King! No, I don't mind serving in the nursery for the next month. I can get through that because I'll be working on training our new volunteers during the week. I'll bake the cake. I'll fold the bulletins. I'll fill in at the last minute to greet at the door.

Yes. Yes. Yes.

Then in the fall of 2019, I said no. For the first time ever. My time was already committed elsewhere, when the last minute request came my way. After countless yeses, spanning almost thirty years, the first no came from my lips. Everything changed.

Fall of 2019 was the last time someone from my church leadership called and asked me to do anything.

Fall of 2019 was the last time I received approval to put together a women's ministry event.

Fall of 2019 I submitted my usual Spring Bible Study information and it was "forgotten" to be included.

It's been two years, without a single word from my church leadership. When I attempted to reach out and offer help during the Covid19 shutdowns, I was dismissed. During the shutdowns, I never heard from the leadership of the church. My graduate was not included in our drive by graduation celebrations. No caravan drove by my home to celebrate my birthday as done for other leaders. When others were showcased for their community service during the shutdown, no one acknowledged the work my family had done. As the church began to open back up, volunteers and leaders were contacted about returning. No one called me. When my family came down with Covid19, my church was missing in action. It's been two years since we last spoke, and it is as if I never existed there.

I have cried and mourned over this for so many days. Tried to justify their actions, and explain it away. Yes, we were in unprecedented times, navigating through new waters. I worked the timeline backwards, looking for the sign of when things changed. It would be easy to blame Covid19, however that didn't impact our area until March of 2020. My heartbreak began in November 2019. The first time I said no.

The signs were present long before. I realized that my relationship with the church was largely transactional. As long as I was saying yes, they were content to let me play ministry. I was never actually a real leader in our church. I was not treated or respected in the same way as the other leaders. I was not valuable, but replaceable when it was no longer working for their purposes.

Can you even begin to imaging what that feels like? To finally see how little you actually mattered to your church family, despite years of dedicated service? All of those years amounted to nothing. The investment of your time, supporting every mission and directive, a constant cheerleader to the vision, only to find yourself not just cast aside but essentially as if you were never there in the first place. Your name blotted from their lips and minds. The only evidence of your existence is the mass email that comes each week reminding you of service times and whatever collection/drive we are participating in this month.

When I said no, I interrupted the transaction.

It's one thing to be a woman who is seeking employment, or position, and to feel rejection. It's another thing to feel as if you were wronged and burn in anger over the injustice of it all. It's an entirely different thing to give all of yourself freely to the vision of the church, never asking anything in return, and to see that were not merely replaceable but forgettable. This was supposed to be my family, my church home. I was supposed to spend out my days here, serving, growing my family here, watching my children marry within these walls, and grow old among the pews. Instead, my heart is broken.

I was not the sheep who wandered, or caused chaos among the pen that required disciple or ejection from the herd. I was the peacekeeper, readily at my Shepherd's side. Neglected and trampled upon, treated with disdain, wounded and left to fester.

It's probably for this very reason, that I will struggle with those in leadership who so easily dismiss the sheep that leave the flock. They try to assert blame upon the person either having an agenda or accusing them of never being part of the flock in the first place. Quick to just let people walk away without any question or self reflection. Refusing to face the hard truth that the person may have not walked out, but instead they were driven out. Facing that perhaps, the Shepherd failed to create a safe place for his wards.

As a leader it is my responsibility to seek after those in my leadership. It is upon my shoulders to reach out, inquire as to why they are leaving, and offer up my best. My best may be learning how I can improve as a leaders, address a toxic situation, or praying over their exit as God brings them to a church that is a better fit. Either way, the onus is on me. The leader.

We do not ask lost children to find their parents, but instruct them to wait right where they are so that their parents can find them. It's the job of the parent to find the child. It's the job of the Shepherd to find the sheep. We, leaders, take the lamp and form the search party.

We are failing as Shepherds, when we leave the gate to the pen open and then blame the sheep for wandering out. We fail as Shepherds, when we push the women out of our doors and then shame them for being wounded."

KARA M. ANGUS
Struggling with a Woman's Offering

"I appeal to you, therefore, brothers, by the mercies of God, to present your bodies as a living sacrifice, holy and pleasing to God, which is your spiritual service of worship (Romans 12:1). That was the message I heard on a Sunday many years ago. The pastor read from the ESV but reminded us that we were all included as "brothers". "Ladies, you just have to read between the lines". I was young and the nuances of gendered language escaped me. But, I clung to something else from that message: the physical body I inhabited was important. What I did as a Christian in that body mattered. My creator valued my mind, body, and spirit and the way it all worked together served as a form of worship. He approved it.

As I moved through teenage years, more urgent messages grabbed my attention. Suddenly the sweet gift of my body seemed to be a real dilemma. *Everything was filtered through the lens of being a 'godly young woman' and ostensibly taught as 'biblical womanhood'. Good girls waited for young men to protect their hearts. Good girls were modest, attractive, quiet, and respectful. Good girls had thin bodies because that proved we understood self control and prioritizing our holy temple. Godly girls were thoughtful and feminine while holding back on true thoughts and interests. There was no talk about spiritual gifts, investing our talents for Christ, ministry opportunities, or growing in spiritual maturity. Becoming a Biblical Woman (not a Christian, an image bearer, or servant of Christ) was serious business with many rules and regulations because much could go wrong.*

What happens when we conveniently forget to tell girls that God has a plan for them and that He has written eternity on their souls too? He has given young women hopes, dreams, and callings. We do not hear sermons about strong women in the Bible. They are an afterthought or minor background character in the story of brave men. Our souls soar to hear a message on Deborah only to crash and burn when we here "God sent her because no good man would step up". Women of the Old Testament who lived out exciting and passionate lives are only referred to by their beauty and charms (or worse as vixens). Women of the New Testament who worked out their faith with fear and trembling, who were discipled alongside the men, who taught and preached, and were called apostles and deacons are discarded as side notes who rarely get an honorable mention.

The good and beautiful message of the Bible, the freedom found in Christ, and the incredible power and strength of the Holy Spirit gets hidden behind a different agenda. Dissonance screams loudly when the gospel we read and the way we are forced to live life out in the pews doesn't come together. Our bodies exist to serve men, to take care of children, provide the food, and feed the people while we are also told those bodies are evil and wrong. We must cover, protect, ignore, shame, and starve them. Interestingly, those all important (and also incredibly dangerous) bodies we inhabit are disconnected from our souls and minds. We are constantly reminded to be at war with our heart, our evil mind, our body, and our wicked emotions. We remain so disconnected from our bodies, our emotions, our hopes, and dreams, and we don't know how to get it back. After all, we are women who rely on our tears. We seduce with our bodies and also have potential to be seduced by dangerous teachings. So we stay quiet. We read on our own. We ignore deep and gaping soul wounds. We accept being invisible. We tell the voices that are screaming out "this is not right" to stay quiet. We quietly resign ourselves to the idea that our gifts aren't really wanted and our sacrifices are not worthy. Our concerns are just "women issues".

For many years, I simply smiled and went on. I prayed against the spirit of anger I prayed for a quiet and submissive heart. Inside I cringed with the young men were invested in, discipled, and trained up in theology as valued future leaders. I heard men complain that a woman would dare to utter a missionary update from behind a pulpit as they spoke with loud, confident voices of all the ways God was calling them to go and serve in the world. My body became useful again to the church as I bore children. I was important. I was contributing to the creation mandate – the sole reason I as a woman existed. After all, the family wins the war against any and all liberal agendas of the world. As one church fellow put it, "we are winning the war against Satan in the bedroom". I absorbed all the pithy statements on how to live out the gospel while I was cleaning dishes and baking a cake. I occasionally crossed paths with other young mothers who had a soul that needed tending to and nobody would do it. I saw other women with thoughts, passions, and gifts who were viewed as a careless afterthought.

Men were automatically invested in and discipled as their church birthright; but no one cared to disciple, encourage, or develop women's gifts and raw talents just below the surface. We are not worth the investment of finding out what God was calling us to beyond raising children, caring for the home, opening our doors to serve the bible study groups, playing music, and providing the food. I went to the marriage conferences, read the books, got the certificate on biblical *womanhood. I thought, "well if this is all there is for me, I am going to to be the best at it I can be". But oh how the darkness and dread closed in on my soul! How I grimaced when I remembered that Jesus gives out gifts and talents and takes it seriously when we bury them.*

Several years ago, I read a book that transformed my life. It talked about Jesus' love for women. It showed how He demonstrated love for women over and over again; and how He taught them, befriended them, rescued them, and saved them. And suddenly, the blurred edges of my confusion, frustration, and deep hurt clicked into focus. Jesus loved me. He died for me. He saved me, and called me. The religious institutions claimed that my ability to make babies and contribute steaming casseroles in disposable pans was my holy and acceptable offering. That the temporary feeding of bellies was all I could offer. Jesus said my holy and acceptable offering was my image bearing self living out faithfully what He placed in my heart to do. My creator values my mind, body, and spirit and the way it all works together serves as a form of worship. He approved it."

REBECCA
Struggling with Standing Up

"I was on staff at a church as the worship pastor for nearly seven years. I was not only the first actual worship pastor, but also the first **woman** *pastor. I grew up in this church, so I knew most of the 500+ people that came every week. The worship had really been ignored for several years. The congregation was* **hungry** *for the move of the Holy Spirit. Most everyone was very welcoming of me into leadership. Very helpful. The staff pastors... yeesh.*

It was such a misogynistic atmosphere. I remember one staff meeting, the senior pastor asked for suggestions, for solutions to an issue. I made a suggestion and no one said anything. Then the Youth pastor said the same thing I did, and the pastor said "Wow! What a great idea!". At the annual business meeting the salaries were post-

ed. I was making half of what the other Pastors were making. When I asked the pastor about it he said, "Well, their spouses are helping them in ministry. Your husband has a job. Their spouses don't."

The thing I wish I had done differently was to stand up for myself. Being raised in a strict church with this type of mentality, made me think it was OK. Be submissive. Don't rock the boat. Stay sweet. When really, it is OK to be paid fairly. It is not OK to be unfairly compensated because your husband has a job.

What wouldn't fly in the secular world should not fly in the church either."

ANONYMOUS

Struggling with Unmet Expectations

"As a woman in ministry, I was not paid the same amount of money for the same work as a man because I had a husband. Even though the church staff knew that he was unemployed due to a layoff. I expected fairness.

As a woman in ministry, I was told numerous times by church staff and lay people that my ideas were not good ones. Even when I was tasked with generating new ideas. I expected support.

As a woman in ministry, when I complained about a parishioner harassing me, I was not believed. One brave elder explored my claim, brought it to the elder board. The parishioner was eventually told to leave. But, I expected to be believed.

Finally, as a woman in ministry, I was told that I could no longer hold that position because "a woman's place is to raise her children and not work outside the home". I expected adherence to US laws.

I am no longer in ministry.

It should be evident as to why."

BEKAH MASON, TH.M.
Struggling with Closed Doors

As much as it hurts to both give and receive this message, finding your ministry niche is frequently more about doors closing than opening. But if you keep going, all those closing doors can eventually lead you outside of the box that you created for the ideas of "calling" and "ministry" and put you in a place you never imagined, faithfully serving Jesus all along the way. My story is just such a tale of meandering with God until I understood what serving him really meant.

When a little girl is raised on Sesame Street, Mister Rogers, and Reading Rainbow, the message received early in life is that you are smart and able and can do anything you set your mind to. After all, that's what the theme song said: "I can be anything! Take a look, it's in a book, a Reading Rainbow, Reading Rainbow!" And oh, did I read some books! Hundreds of books. I couldn't tell you how many Pizza Hut personal pan pizzas I ate through the Book It! Program as an elementary school student.

As the 1980's spilled into the 90's, the messages pumped at me remained largely the same. Women were breaking glass ceilings left and right, Mia Hamm convinced us that she could do anything Michael Jordan could do, and she could do it better. I attended an all-girls school during this time, so alumnae returned regularly to share stories of standing on the shoulders of legends, touching the stars, and aiming still for the moon.

Added to this was a lifetime raised in a conservative Southern Baptist home, where annual offerings are named for women and God calls all sorts of people to do his work. I was ripe to hear a call to do anything God wanted me to do.

So imagine my surprise when I realized there were precious few opportunities for women with my skills and talent to serve in my denomination. As a single woman, there seemed to be even fewer, which was demoralizing because, as I grappled with my sexuality, I saw that singleness would most likely be the path of my life. Despite all of this, I remained convinced of my call to serve God in a full time ministry capacity. I went to seminary to study counseling, but quickly switched to women's studies.

The Women's Studies department at a conservative Baptist seminary is nothing like it is at a secular liberal arts institution. This degree was about doing ministry for and with women in a local church context. Several classes were exact copies of pastoral studies classes, except that the students were all women. We were segregated by gender, learning how to minister to women only. Seemed ineffective for serving in a church, but nothing prepared me for the day we received diagrams of table place settings and instructions for properly folding linen napkins. That day I learned that "women's ministry" was largely event planning, simply feeding into the stereotype that women's ministry is shallow and experiential, devoid of real spiritual development.

As a woman who grew up in the gym and on the ball fields, the idea of serving tea and throwing dinner parties for Jesus was not my idea of serving him. But what was I to do? This was the training set before me to serve. So I continued my classes, gleaning what I could from the women's studies classes and thriving in my co-ed theology and language core classes. As I made my way through seminary, I continued to feel the pull to international mission work, so I began my application to serve with my denomination's mission arm. But when I shared my experience with same-sex attraction, I was told that I wasn't a good fit for international mission work. I then applied with an independent organization as a teacher, but a few months before I was to move, the country I was going to fell into war and all Americans were evacuated.

Why call me, God, to do something that I apparently can't do in any of the known ways of doing ministry? This is when I learned about the doctrine of vocation. It began with a conversation about my own myopic disappointment in finishing seminary only to return to "just teaching" at a Christian school in my hometown. A friend gently rebuked my attitude and approach to teaching Bible and American

History to high school students.

I had fallen for the belief that "ministry" meant full time church or mission work, but I eventually realized that I had the time and influence to pour into students' lives in a way that most student pastors only dream about. Instead of an hour a week at church, I spent anywhere from five to 15 hours a week with students. That's more than most of them spent with their parents. As I studied the concept of vocation, of living out your calling to serve Jesus in whatever place He has you, I realized I wasn't in waiting mode, just wasting time until my ministry opportunity emerged. I was living my call in my everyday life, and God was still working both in and through me.

This is not to say I suddenly developed a perfect contentment in how I was serving. For five years I did serve in a local church as women's ministry director, and was repeatedly frustrated with the inequity between myself and the male staff member who held an equivalent position. We held similar positions, yet he served full time as a paid pastor while I served as a volunteer. After this, I finally stopped shaking the door knob on church ministry, begging it to open. It took nearly a decade of teaching and volunteering before I finally accepted that ministry would simply have a different look for me than traditional paths appeared.

And this was the key lesson for me. As I stopped trying locked doors and started to just faithfully walk through the doors God both led me to and opened, I began to see more of what serving him really meant. It meant faithfully following. It meant serving the one or two people in front of me who were desperate for discipleship. It meant abandoning prideful goals of platform building and listening more than I spoke, recognizing that even teachers still have much to learn. It meant believing to the marrow in my bones that serving the very "least of these" was serving Jesus on a fundamental level of obedience.

Throughout all the trials and missteps, Jesus worked in me so I could see he is working in the small places, with the marginalized and the outcast. So I haven't found a national platform for writing Bible studies and delivering powerful teaching, and I am not serving in a similar way in a local congregation. I am, however, serving Jesus, and serving his people, in ways that I never could have imagined had I written my story for myself.

ALISON DELLENBAUGH
Struggling with a Small Calling

"When I heard the topic of this book, it sounded like my autobiography. Seven years ago, I wrote an article, "When Your Calling Feels Too Small", about my desire to do more in ministry than I'd been able to do in several years of trying. That was the before of my story, and I don't yet have the after! I'm still living in the before. The biggest difference is that now I have a seminary degree, which I hadn't even dreamed of that time. That's been a beautiful gift from God, which I pursued because I had to do something with what He had put in my heart. But as for vocational ministry work, I actually have less than when I wrote the article.

I can't chalk it all up to being female, as I also know males who have struggled in these areas, though it does seem more common among women. For me, seminary was empowering. It's assumed that everyone there will lead in ministry, and I was always treated with respect. And yet, even there, many more women than men are unsure what they'll do with their degrees and may feel more need to justify why they're there. The expectations and opportunities are decidedly different.

Not that there hasn't been progress. Since I wrote that article, I've seen the women's ministry role in my church expand from a volunteer role to a paid pastoral-level role. More women there have served in leadership positions or been visible in other ways. I'm now in the teaching rotation for my mixed-gender adult Sunday School class, which wouldn't have happened then. Women also teach regularly in my conservative seminary chapel, and two of the student body presidents in my time there were female. So I see hope.

Still, my degree, even with honors and an award, has yet to open a door for me vocationally. And I know I'm not alone. I recently prayed with a woman who earned a seminary doctorate last year. Her dissertation focused on the exact area her long-time church has been expanding in—yet to her disappointment, she hasn't been able to speak into that area there.

Perhaps, like me, you can't bear to hear one more person say, "God doesn't want your ability, he wants your availability," when you've been offering your availability for years. You may hear frequent admonitions to use your gifts to serve God, and to use your time wisely for His purposes, but when you try to do just that, all the doors seem closed. Do you ever feel like you've put your whole self on the altar and told God you'd do "anything," and He has rejected the offering? Meanwhile, every month brings another news story about some abuser or charlatan who has led at high levels in the church or ministry, enjoying warm welcomes while you've been waiting on the altar with your heart sold out to God. In my case, the song "Oceans" used to drive me crazy because I felt like He had called everyone else to walk on the ocean while I was either left in a closet or buried in the sand!

Perhaps you've had your motives questioned, or have started to second guess yourself. You may feel guilty for not being content working in the nursery, volunteering for a charity, or serving in a position that doesn't use your primary gifts. You likely do all those things at times. You know they're not in vain and they help build the kingdom of God. You're happy to do them along the way. But you also know God. You've heard His call. You've sought His will in prayer. And deep down, you know it's not "selfish ambition or vain conceit" (Philippians 2:3) driving you. It's a God-given desire (Philippians 2:13) to use the gifts He gave you and the passion He has stoked in you to glorify and serve the Creator and Savior you love. Like the one who desires to be an overseer, you desire a "noble task" (1 Timothy 3:1). You are on a mission from Him. Stand firm, and let your refusal to give up serve as an inspiration to others.

Encouragement for those in the struggle:

Embrace your giftedness and remove the shame. *During my seminary internship, I was trained as a personal giftedness coach. A great takeaway from the process, developed by Bill Hendricks, was the removal of associated shame from our giftedness and motivations. As Hendricks notes, we're often shamed for our natural bents and our motivations. Yet while any of them can be used in sinful or self-serving ways, they're not inherently shameful. This can include even things like a penchant to be in the spotlight. Hendricks points out that without people with some of these motivations, a lot of world-changing things wouldn't happen. As believers, we must take our desires and motivations captive to Christ and His purposes, but we should also use them for Him instead of feeling like we have to hide what makes us tick. When someone tries to shame or diminish you for an inclination you have already submitted to God, cheerfully own the parts of it that are true and refuse to find it problematic. This can defuse the weapons and arguments people try to use against you. Resist the stigma and celebrate how God has wired you! One thing to embrace: your desire to do more in ministry. Unless you're seeking your own glory over God's, your desire honors Him and how He's made you. Embrace who you are and who you can be in Christ.*

God isn't tracking your ministry achievements – He's looking at your heart. *I've had a bad habit of comparing what I've done to what others around me are doing. Some people seem to have extensive ministry resumes while mine is much more bare. Yet God doesn't have a tally sheet of how much ministry you did. He values a sincere heart over a "spectacular ministry" (2 Corinthians 5:12, NLT), and might be more interested in how you treated the store clerk, or whether you nursed your resentment or handed it over to Him, or whether you sought Him while you were excluded from the ministry you wanted to do. Your prayers in your bedroom today may add up to more in eternity than the role you desire might add up to if pursued in your own strength. There are people doing "big things" in ministry right now who won't have a thing to show for it eternally. If the ministry is led* by them instead of God, it isn't serving His purposes and any seeming success adds up to nothing but chasing the wind (Ecclesiastes 2:11). If you are faithful, with your eyes on God, then regardless of what you accomplish in the eyes of the world, you haven't failed.

Look in the right direction. One of the lessons I keep needing to relearn is that ultimately, God opens doors, not humans. It's His approval that counts, not theirs—and His approval is already yours through Christ. You don't have to prove yourself; just lean on Him and persist in prayer.

Don't let anyone encourage you to settle. The decisions you're making about your life aren't just about your life today. They're about the life to come. They're about the current and eternal lives of the people you will touch. Your calling is both a gift and a burden—it matters. If I had taken the advice of everyone who came my way, including the advice of leaders, I'd likely be a very part-time employee for the rest of my life and never have gone to seminary, and would not have accomplished the things I've accomplished along the way. I would have limited what God was ready to do through me. Don't let other voices speak louder into your life than God's. Certainly, don't speak over Him with your own voice, doing what He hasn't called you to do just because you think it would be good. But if He has called, follow no matter what. He is the one you will answer to in the end, and you won't regret it.

Use what you've experienced to make a difference. I recently heard Chuck Swindoll give a powerful message on "the messages in your misfortune." He prayed we would not have an easy path or early success in ministry! Rather, he wanted us to develop fortitude, faithfulness, and empathy. He wanted us to know pain so we'd learn to lean on God more fully. He wanted us to grow in godly perseverance that strengthens character and leads to hope (Romans 5:4). Ultimately, this helps us better minister to others (2 Corinthians 1:4). As one who has known the struggle and endured, use what you've learned to do better for others. Use it to fight for the bride of Christ.

It ain't over when it's over. The thing you desired may have *passed you by, but God can still replace that with something better. He has also proven to be good at resurrection! He can revive a dream that looks quite dead. And even if your whole life ends… as a believer, you have eternal life. What God has prepared in you here and now may come into its own in the eternal kingdom. We won't be floating around playing harps forever; I'm convinced we'll have fulfilling work to do. Your perseverance now and your commitment to your calling will likely influence how you live and serve even in the eternal kingdom of God. None of your preparation or work is in vain.*

God is at work. *Despite the frustrations you've faced, God did not call you to leave you where you are. He called you because He has a plan for you. And what He plans, He will bring to pass. I pray you will soon see those plans falling into place. May your experiences soon add to the hope and the progress He is bringing for the women in His family and for the entire world!"*

AFTERWORD

*"I am convinced that a woman finds her true identity
when she discovers, as I did, that God has broken the
barrier between male and female in Christ. She is released
from having to fit a prescribed mold."*

Lorraine Peters, Our Struggle to Serve, pg. 82

Still Here has been, and will probably remain, one of the most difficult things I have ever written. When I read *Our Struggle to Serve*,
for the first time, I stopped just after Chapter 1. It was too hard to
read, because I was already resonating with the experiences. Pick-
ing it up again, months later, I pushed through the pages. Mixture
of anger, sadness, disappointment, and absolute grief wrecked me
to my core. I could pick pieces from each woman's story and thread
them into my own.

I called a friend, and I read portions to her. She hmm'd in agreement. I snapped a photo of a passage and sent it to another friend,
who messaged me back that she almost threw her phone across the
room. It was in these responses that I realized that I was not alone,
this was common shared experience. When the Lord brings something into your gaze, you begin to see it everywhere. Social media
shares on Twitter from women who were tired of being overlooked,

and under appreciated, suddenly were jumping out to me every time I logged on.

I was reminded of the statistics in *Church Refugees*, as it addressed the exodus of the Dones. Dones are those who have been a large part of the church and leaving because they feel stifled within the walls of the church. Finding their joy in serving in the community, the Dones are living out their calling in a way the brings fulfillment while holding hands with sadness over where they thought they would be. What came to me in the writing of these words was an overwhelming awareness that the church has become so hyper focused on the Nones that they have not ignored the exodus of the Dones... they have missed it completely. Unaware that it has, and continues to happen. The result is that the Dones leave, taking their gifts with them under an enormous emotional toll.

From the book, *Church Refugees (Packard & Hope, pg 14-16)*:

"The dechurched typically struggle with the decision to leave for a long time. - Many, in fact, see leaving the church as the only way to save their faith. - Leaving such a place, then, often means giving up social connections, activity groups, and –perhaps most important – taking on a certain amount of spiritual guilt. Nobody enthusiastically walks away from those things or eagerly embraces feelings of guilt and shame."

...

"They tell stories of frustration, humiliation, judgment, embarrassment, and fear that caused them to leave the church. They remark time and again that they worked diligently for reform within the church but felt the church was exclusively focused on it's own survival and resistant to change. The refugee is a reluctant leaver, packing up only as a last resort. First and foremost and in every way, refugees desire to remain home. They've been forced to flee for reasons beyond their control. At some point, the dechurched decided, in a very intentional way, that they would be better off leaving the church altogether."

...

"Furthermore, they flee the church not because they hate the church. They have, in fact, worked tirelessly on behalf of the church. They flee for their own spiritual safety, to reconnect with a God they feel has been made distant to them by the structure of religion as practiced in organizations."

When the majority of the of those who are leaving are women, who make up the largest percentage of our volunteer force, we are facing a major problem. There are too many talented women, sitting in the pews, waiting for someone to see the value they add to the church. Women with financial prowess and women who understand strategic building. Women with formal training in hospitality, systems, web design, social media platforms, and diversity training that would be an asset to the church are wasting away. Women who run Fortune 500 companies, oversee teams of hundreds, and women who are deeply entrenched in the Word of God are relegated to being Marthas in a world that need Marys seated at the feet only to later go out and proclaim the good news of the risen Christ.

Packard and Hope continue explaining in their work in *Church Refugees* that the people we are losing are the do-ers of our congregations. Said of their research process, *"Almost without exception, our respondents were deeply involved and devoted to their churches up until the moment they left. They are the kind of people who are drawn to activity." (paged 21)* One of these respondents shared, *"It's just hard for me to be a passive worshiper."* While this particular respondent was male, this is the exact feeling high capacity, gifted, women feel in the church.

Being active and involved in central in our pursuit of God, it's not just about being on the team, it is how we worship Him. Exclusion does not just put weight upon our shoulders of disobedience but inhibits our ability to worship to its fullest. A question that resonates from *Church Refugees* is this: *"How can the church possibly hope to survive and thrive as a relevant and meaningful social institution if it keeps spitting out the people who are so dedicated, but feel the need to leave for their own survival; what does that say about the church and it's future?" (Page 25)*

When the Dones leave, they are not walking away from God, but rather running into freedom. Liberated from the confines of the structures of the church, they find freedom to dedicate themselves into the meaningful work. Don't misunderstand that to mean that the Dones are the people who won't do the mundane work that the church needs to get through the day to day operations. As referenced in earlier chapters, it's doing the meaningful work that actually fuels and sustains to do the mundane tasks.

When they leave our churches the spirit of doing goes with them, it engages in community efforts and organizations resulting in fulfillment. Our best and brightest leaders are frustrated that the church structures actively prevent them from doing the work they felt called to do, with more and more walls being put up to inhibit the work. Described as a superficial participation, where the members were not truly active participants but just checking off the to-do list of someone else; there was no actual freedom to shape the community directly. Top down hierarchy of just executing a task list given to volunteers is spiritually alienating versus being inclusive to the various parts of the body, with their various gifts, to be used in various ways. It's narrowed, linear thinking.

Women experience an overwhelming sense of love and appreciation for doing what they've been told, but disdain and irreverence should they want to do anything else. Don't rock the boat or upset the status quo. Don't ask questions, don't challenge, don't assert. Eventually, the person gets tired of being told no and makes the decision to stop trying to be part of that particular body. We do it on our own, or find others who are like minded even if it's outside of the church. When you speak to those who have taken their ministry work into the community, or left their church, you would expect that there would be follow up. Wouldn't you want to know why someone has left? In more experiences than not, it appears the exact opposite occurs.

We Are Builders,
Like Our Father Before Us

We have all heard the description of Christ as a Hebrew carpenter, in fact there are plenty of shirts and graphics over the last twenty years selling the cliched phrase. Carpenters are builders. If we are to be Christlike, we are to be builders. Kingdom builders. We have control over how we build and lead our ministries. There is no reason to stick to some sort of simple model that is peddled from a "how to build a church" manual. Instead, we have the ability and the authority to build exactly what *our* people need versus what everyone else is doing. The Lord will give us the tools, the resources, and the people to get His work accomplished.

As carpenters, we have the ability to deconstruct an old table and make it new. We can build more tables in any shape or size we want. We can build as many tables with as many seats as we desire. We are not limited to some flat-packed Ikea table with assembly instructions made by someone thousands of miles away. Instead, we make the plan and gather our supplies in order to build (or rebuild) to the specifications that the Lord gives us. We can build bigger tables, add more seats, and construct wider doors. We can fill the room with tables, or let them pour out the doors and onto the lawn. We set out the welcome mats.

Lois C. Anderson closes out *Our Struggle to Serve,* with these words: *"I am convinced that the place to begin is within one's own self. We must find peace in our relationship with God as a woman as well as a person. Without that, we will be irritated, frustrated, and belligerent in the church, rather than joyful, patient, and vigorously honest. To be convinced in one's own mind is vital, though there will be ongoing adjustment and growth in this age of transition. --- That should be an exiting adventure, and not the wrangling, loveless debate we find in some Christian magazines and churches. Jesus has the last word: "By this everyone will recognize that you are My disciples, if you love one another." (John 13:35 MLB)"*

She, who comes next, walks in the path you have laid.

Cry out, if you must.

Then muster your strength to do the next thing.

Surround yourself with others who can understand your struggles, but don't allow you to linger there.

We may continue to struggle.

But, we are still here.

She is still here.

And, not going anywhere.

A PRAYER FOR HER

Oh Lord, who hears and sees
Creator of who I was formed to be
Do you hear my cries from my pain
See my cheeks with a teary stain?

You spoke direction into my life
Yet obstacles hinder, I encounter such strife
Did I misunderstand your words to me
And take the wrong path. Did I not see?

Lord, I feel lost and all alone
Unwelcome in my very own home
Speak to my heart, once again, my God
Bring me to the path laid with fresh sod.

A fresh Word.
A clear Call.

I pray that you will surround me.
I pray that you will protect me.
I pray that you will lead me.

Lord, I give you all that I am.